THE TOPICAL TIMES
FOOTBALL
BOOK

CONTENTS

CONTENTS

SENSATIONAL!

The first season

ASK football fans who was the biggest star of last season, and the chances are the majority will plump for Liverpool winger John Barnes.

The 25-year-old England ace enjoyed an incredible season following his £900,000 summer move from Watford.

The transfer itself was not without controversy. Most experts felt that manager Kenny Dalglish was taking a big risk in splashing out so much money on a player whom many felt was too much of an individulalist to fit into a Liverpool style geared to total teamwork.

To further complicate matters, Barnes, the first coloured player to arrive on Merseyside in a big-money deal, became the target of the terracing boo-boys.

Many players would have found the pressure too great. But Barnes proved himself more than equal to the challenge as he set the First Division alight with a season-long display of scintillating skill.

In a matter of weeks, he had made the critics eat their words about the difficulty of fitting in at Anfield.

And he not only silenced the barrackers on the terraces, but brought hordes of new admirers through the turnstiles as supporters up and down the country flocked to watch Liverpool on their travels. "House Full" notices went up at Anfield, too.

As the season unfolded, Barnes made an immense contribution to Liverpool becoming runaway League Champions.

His brilliance also earned him a more regular place in the England line-up.

If there had been any lingering doubts about who was the most exciting player in the land, then those were dispelled when Barnes was voted Player of the Year by his fellow professionals in the PFA and Footballer of the Year by the Football Writers' Association.

When the dust eventually

settled on a marvellous season, Barnes was left to reflect on the impact he had made — and which might never have happened.

For he admits that, if he'd had his own way, he would never have signed for Liverpool in the first place!

Says John, "During my last season at Watford, the 1986-87 campaign, I decided to leave Vicarage Road during the summer. But I never intended to join another English club.

"My big wish was to follow former Liverpool favourite Ian Rush and play in the Italian League.

"So, even though Liverpool made their first approach for me as early as March, I was reluctant to make any kind of agreement with them.

"I think I surprised a lot of people when I expressed my desire to go to Italy. They seemed to think that my game would not suit the close man-for-man marking system they use there.

"But I'm convinced I would have done well playing in Italy. I believe I would have enjoyed the kind of football they play," claims John.

"At home, I watch satellite television and, throughout the season, I see dozens of matches beamed from Italy.

"Whereas many fans immediately think of shirt-pulling and tripping whenever Italian football is mentioned, my view of their game is that it is more skilful than any other country in Europe.

"Unfortunately, my transfer to Italy never materialised. It reached the point where I had to make up my mind between waiting a bit longer and signing for Liverpool," explains John.

"By then, I realised that my dream move to Italy was not going to come off, and that if I was going to stay in England, I couldn't have a better club than Liverpool."

So it proved, as Barnes became an instant hit and played a major role in making the Anfield side the most entertaining title-winners for years.

But he adds, "At first, I really wasn't sure how well I would do at my new club.

"I certainly didn't arrive on Merseyside thinking that I was going to be a world-beater. In fact, I was a little apprehensive.

"Remember, I made my debut at the same time as our other big signing, Peter Beardsley, whom Liverpool had bought from Newcastle for £1.9 million.

"The way I look at it, Liverpool had paid less money for me and I'd come from a less glamorous club, so I had a bit of proving to do.

"The fact I did so is down to the support I received from the rest of the team, and none more so than Peter himself," points out John.

"We quickly struck up a good understanding on the pitch. Some say it was so effective we could have been using telepathy.

"Being an attacker who plays mostly wide, I needed a team-mate I could play off. Someone who would provide the angle required to prevent me from being completely cut off by opponents.

"Peter was the obvious candidate. He's such a busy player, does so much tackling back, and is always available to support me. Throughout the season we used each other to great effect.

Barnes is quick to point out, too, that his new responsibilities brought about a huge improvement in his own game.

He continues, "I know there are many Watford fans who believe I'm exactly the same player I was when I played for them, and have only received so much attention because I'm now playing for a glamorous club, and have better players around me.

"That's just not true. I've become a much better player during the past year, though I confess it does help to have better players alongside you.

"The fact is that Liverpool have been getting so much more out of me than Watford did. The Vicarage Road fans never really saw the best of me. There, I was used as an out-and-out winger, concentrating purely on an attacking role.

"Here at Anfield, however, I've been playing in a much more withdrawn role. Obviously, I tend to be noticed more when I have the ball, take on defenders and become involved around the opponents' penalty area.

"When we're not on the attack, though, I've been paying far more attention to my defensive duties. I now do much more work in midfield than I used to. I've even had spells when I've covered the left-back position.

"That has meant a lot more effort over ninety minutes, but I've relished the extra work and my game has improved."

It's that sort of contribution which, down the years, had led to the famous Liverpool team work — though Barnes believes that is an overworked expression.

He adds, "I agree that one of Liverpool's main strengths has always been the fact that every player works so hard to create a very strong unit.

"However, I don't think the individual talent in the side has always been given the recognition it deserves.

"I believe that recognition finally arrived at the end of last season when the votes were cast for the two Player of the Year Awards.

"I was highly honoured to win on both counts, as I regard those two awards as the highest individual accolades any player could receive.

"More to the point, however, Peter Beardsley, Steve McMahon and Alan Hansen achieved second, third and fourth places in the PFA count.

"In the Football Writers' poll, 96 per cent of the vote went to Liverpool players.

"For me, that sums up exactly how much individual ability there is at Anfield at the moment."

NO CONTEST!
That's why MARK WALTERS joined RANGERS

● When I decided to leave Aston Villa, there was only one club for me — Glasgow Rangers. At the time, I had a straight choice between Everton and Rangers. After I'd met Ibrox manager Graeme Souness and been shown around the stadium, there was no contest.

I must say, though, the clincher for me was the fact I would be playing in European competition. Appearing in Europe is great for a player's reputation. It's been a lifelong ambition of mine to sign for a Continental club.

When I'm a bit nearer thirty, I'd like to try my luck abroad, I reckon my style is more suited to their game.

But I signed a three and a half-year contract with Rangers when I joined them and I mean to make the most of it.

One problem I did encounter when I first arrived in Glasgow, was that I was singled out by opposing fans because I'm black.

I must admit I half-expected the jeering and fruit-throwing I encountered in my first few games.

But the only thing which embarrassed me about it all was the attention it received in the media. I felt it was given more coverage than it was worth.

I've always preferred to keep a low profile on these matters. Firstly because they don't bother me at all, and secondly if some people feel they have to take part in that sort of behaviour, it's surely down to them. Why should I give it any thought?

Once I'm out on the field, I don't notice the crowd, anyway. I have enough problems concentrating on the game in hand and trying to keep my place in the team without worrying about getting stick.

Maybe it was inevitable I would get the treatment because I'm the first black player in the Premier Division — but that's a fact I'm proud of.

The way I see it, I've made history in the Scottish game and that can't be taken away from me. And, while I may be the first, I hope I won't be the last.

Those incidents apart, the risks involved in uprooting myself to Glasgow and playing in a different league were high.

But to be honest, leaving my parents, two brothers and sister behind in Birmingham was made inevitable by the way Aston Villa went about things when my contract was about to expire.

It was hard to leave my family, but Villa meant a lot to me, too. I'd always supported the club and I played with them for seven years. But they didn't offer me new terms until the last day of my old agreement.

I wouldn't accept the club's original terms and they refused to improve them. When Graham Taylor arrived at Villa Park, he tabled an improved offer, but by then I'd decided to look for another club.

I must admit I felt I deserved better. Seven years with one club

may not be a long time in a normal career, but it is for a footballer.

On the whole, I settled in Glasgow very well, although it did take me a while to get used to the 'foreign' food! Within a fortnight of my move, I lost a stone in weight because of a bad stomach upset.

The problem was that I wasn't used to the rich food I was sitting down to in Glasgow hotels. Until then, I'd been used to eating lots of healthy food; white meat, brown bread and the like.

However, in the hotels, I was eating lots of rich food. Lovely as it all was, my system reacted violently to the change in diet.

Eating the right kind of food helps me stay in shape, but I must admit, I let that slip a little in the early days in Scotland.

Something else which took a bit of getting used to was the Glasgow accent. For a couple of weeks, I was pretty bewildered. I'll probably get a bit of stick for saying so, but my team mates Iain Durrant and Derek Ferguson gave me most trouble.

However, we treated it as a bit of a joke, and I can understand them now — most of the time! I must say the Glasgow people are very friendly, and the Rangers support is first class. I get on very well with them.

Playing as a winger in the conditions we sometimes get in Britain, it's inevitable not everything you try will come off. I think the fans know that. If something will work out six times out of ten, I'm quite happy to keep doing it at the risk of looking a bit silly the other four times.

My skills are as much a product of hard work on the practice ground as natural ability. Obviously with things like ball control, you either have the talent or you don't, but I trained hard throughout my time at Villa Park and, if anything, I work even harder with Rangers.

There's no doubt in my mind that the best part of my game is running at defenders. I'm lucky to have a fair bit of pace, too. I'm no Ben Jonson, but I like to think I can get half a yard on most people.

FOOTBALL FIESTA — GERMAN STYLE

● Spectacular stadiums... incessant "Mexican waves"... crescendoes of noise — the European Championships captivated the attention of a whole continent during June as West Germany hosted the tournament second in standing only to the World Cup itself.

The fiesta that was Mexico was transported across the Atlantic to cities like Munich, Dusseldorf and Stuttgart.

The Danish fans arrived with their faces painted like their country's national flag. The Dutch turned up with their Ruud Gullit hats — an orange cap with a mane of black dreadlocks stitched inside. The Irish came with their party songs and unfailing good humour.

For two weeks, Germany lived and breathed the Championships the authorities had worked so hard to stage. There was saturation TV coverage. The streets of every city were festooned with the flags of the competing countries.

The Germans called it the "Europameisterschaft". EM for short. And in terms of its organisation, nothing was left to chance and no expense was spared.

The eight grounds selected each had a minimum capacity of 60,000. Average attendances for the tournament as a whole surpassed that mark. With prices peaking at around £25 for a decent seat, receipts more than justified an outlay which itself was bolstered by sponsorship from some of the world's biggest companies.

Inside, the stadiums were a blaze of colour — with the Dutch leading the way. Holland had more supporters at the Finals than any other nation bar the hosts. And they let themselves be seen and heard in the most spectacular way.

When they played England in the Rheinstadion in Dusseldorf, it seemed every inch of the massive bowl — save the small section

reserved for English fans — had been doused in orange paint.

Ireland's massive following made their own special impact. Initially almost as unpopular as the more loutish section of England's support, the Irish soon convinced everyone that they were different.

They took over the bars and restaurants and the strains of "Molly Malone" soon echoed around whichever city they were in.

On the field, we were treated to some magnificent goals as the best in Europe battled it out over a series of group games based on a league table, then semi-finals and final.

Magnificent electronic scoreboards ran full colour pop videos before the kick-offs — and replays of goals at the end of the games.

There were marching bands before every match, huge airships circling each stadium, battalions of television cameras, Press photographers and reporters to transmit every moment of the occasion around the world.

There won't be another European Championship until 1992. But the World Cup in Italy is just two years away.

Roll on 1990!

HOLLAND — The Champions.

9

HAT-TRICK

A Shambles in Stuttgart, a Disaster in Dusseldorf and a Fiasco in Frankfurt — that's a brief but accurate summing-up of the way the European Championships turned out for England in the summer.

Bobby Robson's squad flew to West Germany with the most impressive qualifying record of all the nations competing. They were second only to the hosts in the betting to lift the trophy.

But after 270 minutes of disappointment and dejection, England were on their way home, without a single point. They had clocked up three successive defeats for the first time in recent international memory.

No one could have predicted the debacle that was to follow as the squad assembled at Luton Airport for their charter flight to Stuttgart and the opening group game against Jack Charlton's Republic of Ireland team.

Behind them was a run of three preparatory matches which brought wins against Scotland and Switzerland and a draw against the impressive Colombians.

So it was with a great deal of confidence that Robson and his men took to the air that Wednesday afternoon in early June.

Installed in a country house hotel set within its own massive grounds the players relaxed before a final practice match against Heilbronn, a local amateur side. It was then that the preparations began to go wrong.

England comfortably beat Heilbronn 4-0, but they sustained injuries to Gary Lineker, Trevor Steven and, significantly, Mark Wright. It was just 48 hours before the opening game of the tournament and with Dave Watson already ruled out with an injury picked up back home, England were down to one fit central defender — Arsenal's Tony Adams.

Manager Robson spent a worrying two days toying with the idea of playing right-back Gary Stevens in central defence, before Wright passed an eleventh hour fitness test and was selected to line up against the Irish.

How England's dreams of glory were shattered.

● Not much to smile about for England manager BOBBY ROBSON (left).

● One of England's few bright spots — BRYAN ROBSON scores against Holland (below).

It was a game everyone expected England to cake-walk. Theoretically it was the easiest game in the group. A two-point cushion for more difficult tests ahead against Holland and Russia.

But Ireland had other ideas. They themselves went to Germany with a superb unbeaten record in run-up matches using a type of long-ball, pressure game perfected at League level by Wimbledon.

Though their line-up contained several players who couldn't hold down places in English First Division sides last season, they played with hearts bursting with pride under their green shirts and shocked England by taking a sixth minute lead through Ray Houghton's header.

The men in white were struggling until half-time. Then they piled on the pressure only to find luck had deserted them. The normally deadly Gary Lineker passed up chance after chance. Irish 'keeper Pat Bonner performed heroics.

The Republic held out and suddenly England were presented with a mountain to climb. Qualification for the semi-

OF DISASTERS!

finals was still possible, but they would have to beat Holland and Russia to make sure of it.

The game against the Dutch was played in a packed Rheinstadion in Dusseldorf, the stands a sea of orange as Holland's supporters outnumbered the English to the tune of around nine to one.

The opening minutes proved crucial, with once again the luck factor working against Robson's men. First Lineker, then Glenn Hoddle struck a post.

But then Marco Van Basten entered the story and with a display of clinical finishing, he rammed a hat-trick past a bewildered English defence, destroying any lingering hope

that there was a way back into the semis for England.

Skipper Bryan Robson managed his side's first goal of the tournament but his team were eliminated after just two games. What a sad way to mark Peter Shilton's marvellous achievement of 100 International caps.

The inquests followed. Shouts went up for manager Robson to resign or be sacked. Fingers were pointed at virtually every member of the side.

All England could do was play for their pride and perhaps do the Irish a good turn as the action moved from Dusseldorf to Frankfurt and the final group game against the Soviet Union.

While England were being demolished by the Dutch, Ronnie Whelan was volleying the goal of the tournament against the Russians. It meant that if England won their final match, they could play a vital part in ensuring the Irish finished first or second in the group to claim a last-four spot.

The mood was one of defiance. In a hotel deep in a pine forest outside the city, England players proclaimed their determination to avoid a whitewash, not only for their own pride, but to help club-mates involved in the other match at Gelsenkirchen.

Alas, it was not to be. England were torn apart by the impressive Soviets, managing a lone Tony Adams goal against three deadly strikes by the Russians. The Irish lost by a single late goal to Holland and they, too, had to book their flight back home.

But what a contrast in receptions when the two squads landed back on home soil. Ireland were met in Dublin by massed crowds, who lined the streets to salute their idols. England's return was greeted with barely a flicker of interest, save that from the critics who were ready to roast them.

Jack Charlton was met by the Irish Prime Minister and given the title 'Honorary Irishman'. He had performed miracles with scant resources. It had been the first time the country had ever qualified for any major Finals and they had exceeded all expectations.

England were left to reflect on another disappointment to follow on from their elimination from the World Cup Finals in Mexico two years earlier.

It meant that in five games in Mexico and three in Germany, they had clocked up just two victories. As the qualifying rounds for the next World Cup Finals in Italy get under way this season, those statistics give worrying food for thought.

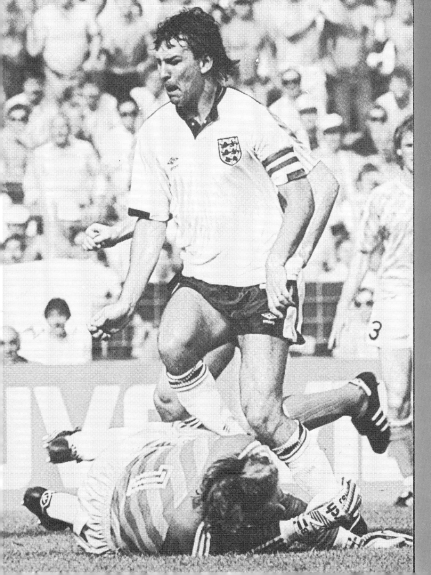

HEROES ALL!

They were rated as underdogs — but Jack Charlton's Republic of Ireland side showed that they had plenty of bite!

Here's a tribute in pictures to the lads in green who left their critics with red faces!

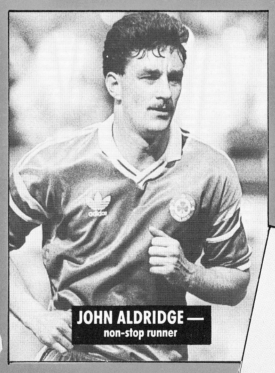

FRANK STAPLETON — courageous captain

JOHN ALDRIDGE — non-stop runner

CHRIS HUGHTON — fast-tackling full back

JACK CHARLTON — inspirational manager

MICK McCARTHY &
KEVIN MORAN —
mighty men in defence

RAY HOUGHTON &
RONNIE WHELAN —
midfielders with the
'goal'den touch

Bryan Robson
As Others See Him

Alex Ferguson

The fact that he is captain of England says everything about Bryan. You don't achieve that sort of honour unless you're very special.

As a skipper, he leads by example. The vast knowledge he has picked up throughout a long career at the highest level, gives him the ability to influence team-mates by what he says on the pitch.

It is very difficult these days for any captain to affect the course of a match by making some sort of change on the park. The game is usually played at too high a speed for that. There isn't much time to assess what's going wrong when you're actually involved.

But Bryan has that ability plus an unbounded enthusiasm which rubs off on those around him.

Neil Webb

Bryan's presence is one big reason for the spirit in the England squad being so high.

Quite apart from his influence on the field — which has been a big help to me in playing alongside him — no young player joining the party for the first time could wish for a better skipper to welcome them.

When I was first selected to represent England, I was terribly nervous, as I suppose most newcomers are. But the moment I reported for duty with the England squad, Bryan was there to greet me. He spent a lot of time with me and generally made me feel at home.

Since then, I've seen him do exactly the same with every new player. With Bryan around, nobody could possibly feel like an outsider.

Gary Stevens

It wasn't easy for Bryan to establish himself as captain of his country.

Four years ago, when England had failed to qualify for the European Championship Finals in France, he shouldered much of the responsibility because, along with Ray Wilkins, he was regarded as the engine room of the side and the man expected to contribute most to the team's performance.

But he never once let that set-back affect him, and it's a tribute to his greatness that he emerged as the player round whom manager Bobby Robson has built his current international team.

All over the world, the first player the kids approach for an autograph is Bryan Robson — simply because he is a world class player and such a wonderful ambassador off the field.

He's the type of player I would recommend any youngster to look up to and use as a model to follow.

Peter Beardsley

I can't imagine the current England side being successful without Bryan in the team.

He's a great leader both on and off the field — tackles well, creates chances, scores goals and defends brilliantly.

It was easy for me to join the England squad with Bryan as its captain, having spent five months with him as a Manchester United player back in 1982.

I made only one Milk Cup appearance for the club, but from the moment I arrived at Old Trafford it was clear that I could turn to Bryan if I had any problems.

He's the sort of captain whom even the youngest reserve player at Old Trafford could phone at any time of the day or night and tell him his worries.

Bryan might not have the answer, but I know he'd do everything he could to help.

Kenny Sansom

Bryan can win or save a game. He's so versatile, he plays equally well at the back or going forward. That's an asset which England have never really used but one which we have up our sleeves if necessary.

I was already in the international set-up when Bryan joined us, so I've watched him develop into the great player he is at that level.

Right from the start, it was clear he was going to be a bit special. His enthusiasm, both in matches and in training, was boundless — and he learned very quickly. That's something you have to do if you're going on to captain your country in a World Cup campaign.

There are several young players in the international squad who have the makings of a future England captain. But Bryan's determination is such that I'm sure it will be some years before he is ready to give up the job.

In the meantime, those youngsters could do a lot worse than study Bryan as the perfect example of how the job should be done.

Chris Waddle

There's one word which sums up Bryan Robson — he's a winner.

As a player, he knows what he wants and never loses the determination to achieve his objective. He plays the same way from the first minute of a match to the last.

As a captain, he's the inspiration behind his team and seems to have the knack of getting every member of the side going no matter how he is playing himself. When his team is behind, Bryan is the one who lifts them.

I don't think that Bryan's will-to-win has ever varied at any point in his career. Nearly every player I know goes through a spell at some time when his confidence is at a low ebb. I don't recall Bryan ever experiencing that.

He has a great scoring record for a midfield player. Bryan's knack of arriving at the penalty area at exactly the right moment is brilliant. There isn't a player in the country who does it so well.

IT HAPPENED LAST SEASON

1. **One First Division match boasted eleven goals. Name the teams involved and the final score.**

2. Which Luton Town player was called up for both England and Northern Ireland before choosing the latter?

3. **There was one ever-present in all competitions for Champions Liverpool. Name, please.**

4. Port Vale provided the biggest Cup shock of the year, beating Spurs 2-1 in the FA Cup. Can you name the Vale goal heroes?

5. **Which Third Division player scored a hat-trick on his debut for Eire?**

6. Which First Division goalkeeper found himself on the substitutes' bench on the last Saturday of the season?

7. **During the course of the season there was only one million pound transfer. Can you name the player and the club he joined?**

8. There were two penalties missed in Cup Finals at Wembley. Can you name the culprits and their clubs?

9. **Which two English sides each put ten goals past the opposition in League games?**

10. Which Everton star scored the goal which brought Liverpool's 29-game unbeaten run to a close?

11. **Which Scottish Premier Division goalkeeper scored direct from a kick against Morton?**

12. Who was Terry Venables' first signing as manager of Spurs and who then went on loan to Swansea City?

13. **Which four teams contested the play-offs for a First Division place?**

14. In the international against Holland at Wembley an England player scored for both sides. Name, please.

15. **Which former Rangers player did Derby County rescue from Spanish side Seville?**

16. Which side ended the season as top scorers in the Scottish Premier Division?

17. **Who managed Millwall to the Second Division Championship?**

18. Which striker scored three goals in his first three games in a West Ham United shirt to help the club out of relegation trouble?

19. **Chelsea used four different goalkeepers. How many can you name?**

20. Which side knocked Glasgow Rangers out of the European Cup and which country did they represent?

21. **What was Frank McAvennie's transfer fee from West Ham to Celtic?**

22. Which manager had spells at two different clubs last season only to see them both relegated?

23. **Which Scottish team was first to win promotion?**

Answers on Page 116

THERE WERE PLENTY OF MOMENTS TO REMEMBER IN 1987-88.
HOW MANY CAN YOU RECALL?

● **TREVOR PEAKE** *Coventry City*

17

FIGHT
TO BE FIRST!

Liverpool's PETER BEARDSLEY battles desperately to get to that ball before Everton keeper NEVILLE SOUTHALL. But a courageous dive and a safe pair of hands make sure the keeper comes out the winner —this time!

● **MIRANDINHA** *Newcastle*

19

● The players who attend the Football Association's rehabilitation and sports injury centre at Lilleshall call it 'Colditz'. The staff will tell you that it's an affectionate tag.

Talk to a soccer star who has endured a six-hour session including time on the notorious 'Hill' and 'Grand National' and you'd be hard pushed to detect any hint of affection in his voice!

However, speak to them when they motor out through the gates, with the prospect of first-team action once again, and the player who limped into Lilleshall with a question mark over his future will recommend 'Colditz' to anyone.

The comparison with the infamous German prisoner-of-war camp is understandable. Despite modern annexes, the main body of the centre is an imposing, but cold-looking former hunting lodge.

It is here that footballers and other sportsmen slog their way back to fitness. The rehabilitation centre opened its doors in September 1986. At first most of the equipment lay unused as clubs shied away from the new centre, preferring instead to keep a close eye themselves on their injured stars.

The trickle of users grew as word spread that Lilleshall was indeed a success. After intensive treatment players with horrendous injuries or mundane

AGONY
BUT IT'S WORTH IT!

LILLESHALL — WHERE CRIPPLING INJURIES ARE CONQUERED BY HARD WORK AND SKILLED HELP

niggling ones, were well on the road to recovery.

Head physiotherapist Graham Smith and his assistant Philip Newton, plus four full-time physios, have a wide range of injuries to deal with.

Severe fractures, dislocations, snapped Achilles tendons, complicated groin strains, muscle ruptures and shattered ligaments are some of the problems faced by the team at Lilleshall.

It's a hard long slog to get the injured limbs back to full working order. Players who have developed a limp following surgery, are even taught to walk properly again!

The main gymnasium was originally built as a dance studio. The sprung floor and full-length mirrors down one side are ideal for players to study their walk and correct any faults.

The gym houses an impressive array of medical equipment both simple and technologically advanced. On one hand there's a hydraulic weight machine that taps out a graph so the patient can see the progress he's making on a knee that needs to be worked back to full bend. On the other is a simple medicine ball, held between the ankles whilst rolling over in order to build up damaged groin muscles.

Injured players are supervised strictly by the six-man team. They are divided into three groups — newcomers, intermediates and those on the last lap of recovery.

Most players are on a five days a week residential course, working from 9 a.m. to 5 p.m. Length of stay is dependent on the severity of the complaint.

On arrival, a player's injury is assessed and a rehabilitation programme designed for the specific problem is then drawn up.

Assessment also takes place in the Human Performance Department. Computerised treadmills, blood analysis and weight machines churn out charts to reveal a patient's level of fitness throughout his stay. A player can then see the progress he's making.

A typical week at Lilleshall is certainly no picnic.

Assistant physio Philip Newton explains the arduous programme he has to bully and cajole patients through. He pushes them to their limit without going over the top and further damaging an injury.

"A number of sessions during the day are spent on individual programmes. Here a player will work on the schedule set out for his injury," says Philip.

"Slotted into their day, depending on what their injury will allow, will be time spent on swimming, cycling, walking, running, the 'Grand National' and the 'Hill'.

"The sessions in the pool aren't a splash about for fun," emphasises Philip. "It's an hour of non-stop work. There are relay races in pairs where one treads water whilst the other does a length. We have both walking and running races in the pool and water polo.

"The lads are sent out on bike rides of up to 13 miles through the grounds and the surrounding countryside. We have a number of mountain bikes for getting over rough terrain.

"Long distance walking and running is also included in the programme," adds Philip. "Then we have the 'Grand National'. The gym is turned into a course of around 20 different exercises. It is a real endurance circuit. Forty-five minutes of continuous exercises.

"The 'Hill' is another 'popular' session. We have a short, steep natural mound in the grounds here and the players have to run up and down it.

"Even in the summer it's ankle deep in mud," points out Philip. "I think our groundsman waters it every day!"

It's tough and no place for shirkers, but the FA's rehabilitation centre has worked minor miracles for some players.

England and Rangers' defender Terry Butcher, Liverpool's Jim Beglin, Kevin MacDonald and Jan Molby, Everton's Kevin Sheedy and Leeds' Brendan Ormsby to name but a few, have all had good reason to thank the centre.

BRENDAN'S BATTLE

One player who owes a lot to Lilleshall is Leeds United's BRENDAN ORMSBY. This is how he fought to get fit.

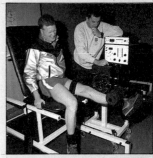

● Head physio Graham Smith supervises Brendan on the muscle treating machine.

● Pedalling nowhere fast! Muscle-building exercises on the exercise bike.

● Hard work — but Brendan can still smile!

● On your bike! One more step in the long slog back to fitness.

● **STEWART McKIMMIE** *Aberdeen*

STRE TCH!

Southampton's COLIN CLARKE (left) competes in a muscle-straining challenge with NOEL BLAKE (Portsmouth).

23

● **ALAN SMITH** *Arsenal*

24

● **KEVIN DRINKELL** *Norwich City*

25

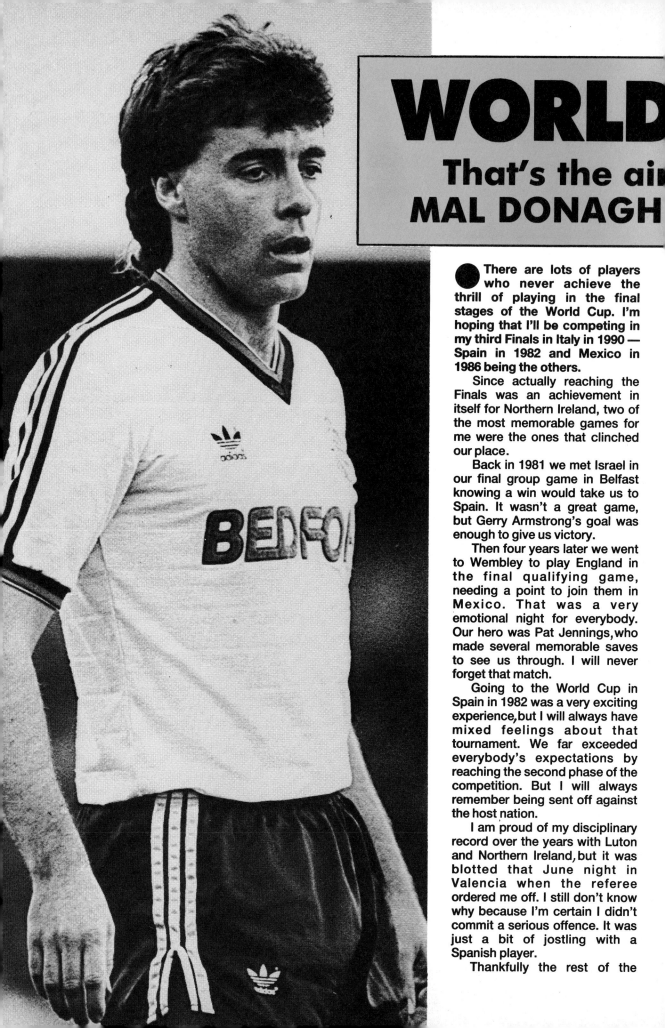

● There are lots of players who never achieve the thrill of playing in the final stages of the World Cup. I'm hoping that I'll be competing in my third Finals in Italy in 1990 — Spain in 1982 and Mexico in 1986 being the others.

Since actually reaching the Finals was an achievement in itself for Northern Ireland, two of the most memorable games for me were the ones that clinched our place.

Back in 1981 we met Israel in our final group game in Belfast knowing a win would take us to Spain. It wasn't a great game, but Gerry Armstrong's goal was enough to give us victory.

Then four years later we went to Wembley to play England in the final qualifying game, needing a point to join them in Mexico. That was a very emotional night for everybody. Our hero was Pat Jennings, who made several memorable saves to see us through. I will never forget that match.

Going to the World Cup in Spain in 1982 was a very exciting experience, but I will always have mixed feelings about that tournament. We far exceeded everybody's expectations by reaching the second phase of the competition. But I will always remember being sent off against the host nation.

I am proud of my disciplinary record over the years with Luton and Northern Ireland, but it was blotted that June night in Valencia when the referee ordered me off. I still don't know why because I'm certain I didn't commit a serious offence. It was just a bit of jostling with a Spanish player.

Thankfully the rest of the

UP HAT-TRICK
f Luton and Northern Ireland's
s he is setting his sights for 1990

team made up for my disappointment that night by scoring a famous victory over Spain, with Gerry Armstrong again scoring the winner.

Although I was bitterly disappointed at being sent off, I was still proud of the way we played throughout the tournament.

Four years later in Mexico we didn't do quite so well but it was still a very enjoyable experience. It was then that I realised a great ambition by playing against Brazil.

Brazil might not have won the World Cup . . . but they were still a very special team and I loved every minute of the experience of playing against them. I don't think any of us will forget the great goal that their full-back Josimar scored against us. Not even Pat Jennings could stop a shot that was hit with such power. It simply flew past him.

In Mexico we were knocked out in the first stage of the competition but I reckon we'd still done well. We are only a small country and can't realistically expect to win the World Cup. But we certainly enjoyed ourselves having a go.

It is hard to believe that I now have the chance to qualify for a third World Cup. I could only dream about such things when my career started. In fact I didn't even think that I would become a full-time professional footballer.

I was playing part-time for Larne in Northern Ireland as a teenager while working full-time in a clerical job for the Post Office. That suited me fine and it's really the way I expected it to stay.

Then, out of the blue, Luton Town asked me to go to England and play for them. I decided it was too good a chance to miss even if I was settled at home.

Looking back now I can say that it was the right decision. I've had ten very happy years at the club, although a lot has changed in that time.

For some years we were only a Second Division club but over the last few years we've established ourselves in Division One. And of course winning the Littlewoods Cup last season was a great boost.

But the last few seasons have also seen a bit of controversy around Luton.

It all started when the club decided to instal a plastic pitch at Kenilworth Road. That sort of surface had already proved unpopular at Queen's Park Rangers' ground but for Luton it made economic sense.

It certainly made a big difference to the way we played the game. In the winter you

● **GERRY ARMSTRONG — scorer of vital goals.**

expect to play on a lot of muddy pitches but ours is the same all the year round.

Players who play on plastic just a couple of times a season find it difficult to get used to, but when you know the surface well it can really help improve your game. My all-round game has certainly benefited — particularly my control and passing.

The second major controversy came after our pitch had been invaded by Millwall fans at an F.A. Cup quarter-final match. Soon after that the Luton board decided all away supporters should be kept out.

At first it was a bit strange not to hear away supporters. But to be honest I'd never taken much notice of them anyway. The fans have never scored a goal against us!

Actually I've never been one to take much notice of a crowd at a game home or away. When you walk out at Old Trafford or Anfield you can sense the fans around you. But as soon as the whistle blows it's just another game, and I must have total concentration on what I'm doing.

When you are a defender you have to be alert throughout the game. One mistake could be fatal for the team. That's certainly true of my position at Luton where I stick mainly to defensive duties. For Northern Ireland I get the chance to attack a bit more.

It might not seem very glamorous to be a defender. But in my position I've played over 400 League games for my club and more than 50 for my country, including several in World Cup competition. And that's a record to be proud of.

● **JOHN GREGORY** *Derby County*

GET WELL TEL!

For Rangers and England central defender Terry Butcher, season 1987-88 was clouded by a broken leg which put him out of the game for several months.

It meant that most of the season Big Tel was faced with a long, lonely slog back to full fitness. But one bright spot for the big defender was the shoal of get-well messages which fans and players sent to him from all over the country. Testimony to the high regard that Terry Butcher has earned by his resolute displays for club and country.

Welcome to White

Meet Willie Morgan — the voice of Tottenham Hotspur

● "Welcome to White Hart Lane — world famous home of the Spurs!" The voice of announcer and disc jockey Willie Morgan is as well known at Tottenham as the skills of England star Chris Waddle.

Willie Morgan is a link between the club and the paying public. His pre-match record shows keep the fans entertained, and his announcements keep them informed on all club matters. But his involvement goes much deeper than just his match-day broadcasts.

He helped put Spurs and England discs into the hit parade — and made recording stars out of Glenn Hoddle and Waddle.

Away from football, Willie Morgan is a promotions executive in the music business.

A dual love of football and pop music helps give Willie the perfect background for his part-time job at White Hart Lane. A season-ticket holder for years,

he took over behind the 'mike' in 1980. But his first link with pop music and football was four years earlier.

"I was taking singer David Cassidy around to different appointments in 1976, as part of my job with a record company," recalls Willie.

"We were at the BBC for an interview with Ed Stewart on his Junior Choice show. When Ed asked David what he was doing for the rest of the day, David said he would like to see a football match — at Tottenham.

"We ended up in the directors' box at White Hart Lane. I bet it's the only time there has been a bunch of screaming teenage girls trying to climb into the directors' box!"

A couple of years later Willie met the (then) Spurs physio Mike Varney, who was preparing a tape on the treatment of sporting injuries.

That led to more contact backstage at Spurs and an

eventual offer to take over the microphone at White Hart Lane.

"I had been a hospital radio DJ for several years, so I had some experience," says Willie. "I took over the job in August 1980, the debut match of Steve Archibald and Garth Crooks.

"I was surprised to find the equipment at the ground was not up to the standard of hospital radio — and that there was no view of the pitch from the 'studio'.

"It was a bit tricky, because to be able to follow the match and announce goalscorers and substitutions, I had to leave the studio to watch from the stand.

"Everything went O.K. in my first game, but in my second match I left the mike switched on by mistake when I went to watch the game," Willie goes on.

"In the middle of the play there suddenly came the deafening sound of a telephone ringing right round the ground. You could almost see the players saying 'It's for you hoo . . .'.

"It suddenly dawned on me that it was the telephone in my studio, and I had to shoot back and switch off the mike before answering the phone," confesses Willie.

"Luckily, Spurs were about to demolish the old stand and build a marvellous new one and I was fully consulted on what was needed for the public address announcer.

"I was provided with up-to-date turntables and a good view of the pitch. I now have a very well-equipped studio in front of the main stand."

It was a good time for Willie Morgan to start his association with Spurs because that season the team went to Wembley for the F.A. Cup Final.

"Even before the semi-final was played, the decision was made to release a record in time for the Final", reveals Willie.

"I'd met singing duo Chas and Dave through business

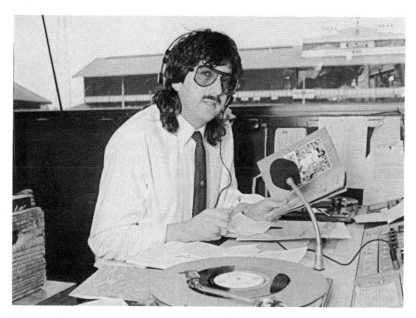

Hart Lane!

dealings and knew they were great Spurs fans. So they were approached to write a song, and they come up with 'Ossie's Dream'. In honour of Argentinian star Ossie Ardiles, of course.

"The record sold 190,000 copies and reached number five in the hit parade. As it crept up the charts, the Top of the Pops producer became interested. He wanted the team on the show in Cup Final week, and that was a headache for me.

"Manager Keith Burkinshaw had put a six o'clock curfew on the team for that week — and Top of the Pops was a live show which began at seven-thirty," explains Willie.

"I told Keith that a trip to the studios would be a great relaxation for the Final. He said it would be okay — as long as it was finished before six o'clock.

"I then persuaded the BBC to record the Spurs team at rehearsal during the afternoon, and then use the recording in the live show.

"But that meant there was a shortage of pop fans in the studio to create atmosphere during the recording. That's why coach Peter Shreeve, physio Mike Varney and myself were to be spotted in the background on Top of the Pops waving Spurs scarves!" laughs Willie.

"In fact, I was so nervous that while we were swaying from side to side, waving the scarves like a football crowd, I became so totally out of time that I stuck out like a sore thumb.

"For months afterwards the video of that show was regular viewing on the Spurs coach to away matches, and my performance always got a laugh from the players.

"The following year, Spurs reached Wembley again. Chas and Dave came up with a great song 'Tottenham, Tottenham, we're going to do it like we did last year'.

"That also entered the charts.

I was called in, also, as an adviser on the England team's World Cup record, and that did very well," said Willie.

"One week on Top of the Pops there were three football records — Scotland, Spurs and England. Steve Archibald went into the record books as the first man to sing on two different records on the same Top of the Pops show — closely followed by Glenn Hoddle and Ray Clemence.

"Glenn has always loved singing. He once gave me a tape he'd made of an Elton John song. I was staggered by his ability. It was not an easy song to do, with a wide range of notes," explains Willie.

"I told Glenn to give up football and do something worthwhile — like pop singing! In 1982 Glenn did a solo for the England team's L.P., and I knew I had to take him seriously as a vocalist.

"In 1986 he gave me another tape to listen to. Glenn and Chris Waddle had recorded a song called 'Diamond Lights'. All my experience in the record business told me it had the makings of a hit.

"'Diamond Lights' shot into the top 40, in at number 30. Top of the Pops began to take an interest again.

"It was arranged that Glenn and Chris would appear on the show the day after a match at Wimbledon, a time they would normally have 'free'.

"Again I ran into a hitch," explains Willie. "Both players were injured and missed the Wimbledon match. That meant training next day and receiving treatment for their injuries.

"In desperation, I obtained permission for both players to report extra early at the training ground, so they could leave in time to go to the Top of the Pops studio."

Being the D.J. is only part of Willie Morgan's job at White Hart

Lane. He has to be there as soon as the gates open to the public, because he's the man who has to co-ordinate any evacuation of the ground in an emergency.

"I had to learn the safety regulations, and all the procedures in the event of a fire or bomb scare," says Willie.

"There are various 'coded' messages I have to put out to alert stewards and turnstile operators without alarming the public. Of course, I'm under the control of the senior club officials and police."

Before the ban on English clubs playing in Europe, Willie endeared himself to foreign visitors at White Hart Lane by reading out a welcome message in the language of the visiting side — even though he couldn't understand a word!

"From the start I felt it was a nice touch to welcome teams in their own tongue," he says. "I used to approach foreign airline companies to get someone to translate a welcome message — and trusted them not to play a joke on me!

"King Olaf of Norway once attended a match at White Hart Lane. During the afternoon I played a record of the Theme from Harry's Game, by Clannad.

"After the match one of the King's aides came into the studio. 'I must get a copy of that record — the King loves it,' he said.

"I wasn't going to let go of my version because it's a record I play at the end of a game if Spurs have lost — it's a sad, haunting sort of sound. But I put them in touch with the record company, so I presume there's now a copy of that disc in the King's palace in Norway.

"As a Spurs fan, I don't like having to play it much at White Hart Lane. But I know they have to lose sometimes, and I like to match the music I play to the mood of the occasion.

"As far as I'm concerned football and pop music go hand-in-hand. Playing my favourite tracks, and watching my favourite football team — there's no better way to spend a Saturday afternoon," declares Willie Morgan.

● TIM BREACKER *Luton Town*

● **GARY STRODDER** *West Ham United*

● **GERAINT WILLIAMS** *Derby County*

34

WHY SUNDERLAND'S
IAIN HESFORD HAS OPENED UP
HIS SCRAPBOOK AGAIN.

Since the day I signed for Blackpool as a youngster over ten years ago, I've kept a scrapbook. In it I've carefully filed every little bit of information about me that's appeared in print.

Every bit, that is, bar the 'cuttings' which should have covered the events of the season before last.

Today, when I flick through my scrapbook, the pages reserved for that particular chapter are blank!

That they will always stay that way serves as a vivid and painful reminder of the worst period in my life.

Season 1986-87 was the one when I reached such a low ebb that I could easily have jacked-in the game altogether. Certainly the thoughts crossed my mind.

The end of that term, my first at Roker Park, had seen Sunderland relegated to the Third Division for the first time in their long and proud history.

Suddenly, the great move I'd made

and Steve was a very fine Rugby League player. But both have now finished playing.

They pointed out how much they missed competitive sport. How much they'd love to be in my position of playing and earning a living from football.

Appreciating their loss put everything back into perspective. What they'd suffered made me aware I was guilty of feeling too sorry for myself.

I'll always have Bob and Steve to thank for not only encouraging me to pick up the threads of my career, but also to do so again with Sunderland.

What also bucked me up no end was the surprising number of letters I started to receive from Sunderland fans.

In the circumstances I could have expected a load of the abusive variety. Instead, a lot of the mail I received was amazingly supportive.

One in particular last season really showed the difference just a few short months can make in football.

By this time I was back in the first team and the writer made it perfectly clear that he'd been one of my most severe critics in the previous campaign.

Because of this, he explained, he felt obliged to let me know that by coming back and doing so well I'd made him eat his words.

That confession, plus a few others in the same vein during last term, meant a lot to me. These letters made me glad I'd decided not only to carry on playing, but to do so at Roker Park.

In fact, those letters now have pride of place in my scrapbook. Last season went so well for me that I again opened up my personal collection of career highlights.

But, of course, the very best thing of all to happen to me last season was being part of the line-up which won promotion, taking Sunderland back to Division Two at the first attempt.

That really was something to enter in the scrapbook!

NO MORE BLANK PAGES!

from Sheffield Wednesday barely nine months earlier had turned into a nightmare . . . and not just because of the club's disastrous slide to relegation.

What hurt even more was that during the campaign I'd become one of the main 'whipping-boys' of the Wearside fans. I ended up on the transfer-list after being widely criticised for a series of blunders!

Now, I don't deny I was guilty of some crucial mistakes during that campaign. But probably the biggest error I made was being too honest about it.

Things seemed to snowball after I had the courage to accept blame for the first couple of errors. From then on, too many folk appeared too willing to blame me for just about everything.

The pressure was almost unbearable at times. I was even left carrying the can when some of the goals we conceded weren't even my fault.

But, whatever the rights and wrongs of that, I ended the campaign on my knees and all but counted out.

I returned to my home town of Blackpool for a summer break, wondering not just whether I could ever face going back to Sunderland again, but whether I actually had any future in the game.

I'd taken such a mental buffeting that I didn't really know which way to turn. But the thought of packing in completely was on my mind.

That was the point when my family, particularly my brothers Bob and Steve, stepped in to make it clear they thought I was wrong to think like that.

Bob played Rugby Union for England

● **TREVOR STEVEN** *Everton*

Luton's MICK HARFORD, backed up by Arsenal's TONY ADAMS and Luton's LES SEALEY, leads the way in this well-drilled routine!

3 2 1

LIFT OFF!

● I thought I'd found the ideal job for the rest of my life when I joined the police force on my 18th birthday.

Six months' training and a year as a 'beat' constable didn't change my mind. I was enjoying a career which was giving me a good deal of job satisfaction. Each day was exciting. You never thought about looking at your watch.

I felt I had a future in the force and my football was confined to playing for a Sunday League team. Then I was asked to have a trial for Chesterfield. I spent a year with their youth team while continuing my police duties.

Then the present Derby County boss, Arthur Cox, took over as manager at Saltergate and asked me to sign as a full-time pro. At that point I had to make a decision.

I loved police work, but the one thing I liked more was football. In fact, even as a copper, I'd always wanted to be on duty at a big match but had never been given the chance.

Not many people are given the opportunity to become a professional footballer and I knew that if I turned it down, I would have always wondered what might have been. And I had

'KEEPERS

a little security in that my Chief Superintendent had hinted that if things didn't go well, I would be welcomed back to the force.

As it happened, it couldn't have worked out better! Arthur Cox threw me straight into the first team after just a couple of months' pre-season training. Sixteen games later I was on my way to Liverpool!

To say I was surprised is an understatement. I was very much a learner, yet here was the top club in the country wanting to sign me.

The Anfielders wanted me as understudy to Ray Clemence, then the England 'keeper. It meant reserve team football, but a regular spot as one of the substitutes for European matches.

I didn't have much chance to think about it. Arthur Cox told me I was signing and I didn't argue. He is such a dominating character that 19-year-olds with a couple of months' first team experience don't argue with him!

More seriously, however, I looked on the transfer to Liverpool as a chance to have the apprenticeship I never had at Chesterfield. The one thing I knew I lacked was a grounding at reserve team level.

I reckoned that Anfield was as good a place as any to be given that grounding, especially as I had the bonus of working with Ray Clemence. I hoped his good habits would rub off on me.

In the end I was there for four and a half years and played just five first-team games. Despite all the advantages of being with a club like Liverpool — such as collecting a European Cup-Winners' medal in my first season — it eventually became

for lengthy periods of matches, such was their dominance of the Central League.

As a result you can become a bit complacent. You have the odd save to pull off but if you do, people simply say that's what you are paid for. If you make a mistake, doubt is cast on your ability to step up to the senior side. It's a no-win situation.

So, towards the end of the 1980-81 season, I asked Bob Paisley, the manager at the time, for a transfer. He said I could go when they found a replacement. Just after that the club signed Bruce Grobbelaar.

Then Ray Clemence dropped a bombshell and asked for a move himself. He went to Tottenham and the club was left with just Bruce and myself. So I wasn't able to leave after all.

Bob Paisley decided to start the following campaign with Bruce in goal as they had paid a substantial fee for him. But if it didn't work out I was to get my turn in the first team.

Bruce did have a shaky spell midway through that first season and I thought I might have been given my chance. But the boss stuck by Bruce and he has since developed into one of the country's top 'keepers. I again

At the end of my contract I signed for Coventry City and I hope in my four years at the club I have given full value for the £72,000 paid for me.

Certainly in terms of matches played that would seem to be the case. I finished last season having never missed a game for the club, something I'm proud to say has been true at every club I've been at.

People have come to class me as one of the best uncapped 'keepers in the League. I'm very flattered by that — although I wish I had been 'capped'.

I've been on the fringes of the England squad and was put on stand-by duty at one stage last season. It may still happen for me. I'll just keep on hoping.

I was 31 in September and while that might seem old for an outfield player, goalkeepers these days have a longer life than the rest.

I'm reaping the benefit of the achievements of such as Peter Shilton, Ray Clemence, Pat Jennings and Phil Parkes. They have been so dedicated, they have proved that even in their mid and late thirties they can play at the highest level.

In fact, there seems to have been a complete shift in policy

LAST LONGER NOW!

STEVE OGRIZOVIC explains why.

evident I'd have to leave for the good of my career.

I hesitate to criticise anything Liverpool did. But because Ray Clemence was such a naturally talented 'keeper I didn't feel the goalies at the club were worked hard enough in training.

I thrive on hard work. That's probably why I progressed so quickly under Arthur Cox, who is a very strict taskmaster. But as a reserve 'keeper at Liverpool you could be virtually unemployed

put in a transfer request and ended up at Shrewsbury Town, a move I now consider to be the best of my career.

Graham Turner, who is now at Wolves, was in charge and he said right away that I needed sharpening up. I agreed and he gave me the opportunity to work morning and afternoon if I wanted to.

I had two good years at Gay Meadow and it was just the experience I'd been looking for.

by managers of clubs, particularly those outside the First Division.

In my younger days, bosses seemed to go for an experienced back four, but were happy to blood a young 'keeper behind them. Now clubs use an old hand between the posts but play young defenders in front of him.

A 'keeper's career has been prolonged as a result. That's why I reckon I still have a good future in the game.

● GERRY FORREST *Southampton*

● **ALAN McINALLY** *Aston Villa*

41

An Offer I Couldn't

●BEFORE I became a Manchester United player, I was attracting the interest of a number of talent scouts from various clubs.

As a 15-year-old, I captained both the Wigan and Lancashire junior teams, and many of our matches were attended by club representatives weighing me up as a future prospect.

The twist is that, had those scouts followed up their interest, I might not have played football at all!

Those spies were working for Rugby League outfits, and it was my performances as a stand-off half that interested them.

Twice a week I played for those representative sides, as well as for my school team. I was also a regular attender at Central Park, home of Wigan Rugby League Club, my local team. And whenever I made a trip to Wembley, it was always for the RL Challenge Cup Final.

So how did a young lad steeped in Rugby League tradition became a First Division goalkeeper and an England Under-21 internationalist?

The simple answer is that, as a schoolboy, I devoted all my spare time to both sports. In addition to being a member of those rugby teams, I also played football for my school and local boys' club side, though in those days I was a centre-forward.

Eventually the day arrived when I had to choose between the two codes. But, because it was Manchester United who wanted to sign me, that decision was just a formality. There was no way I could have chosen any path other than the one to Old Trafford.

If I'm truthful, I'd say that football is the sport I'd always wanted to follow. But when you live in Wigan, it's impossible not to be caught up in the passion for the oval ball game. It's a rugby town. Everyone who lives there follows the fortunes of the local club.

My family are big Wigan fans, especially my Dad. He goes to watch them regularly, and that's how I started attending matches.

Although I occasionally travelled to Manchester to watch United or City, it was much easier to pop along to Central Park for the rugby matches.

Wigan then were not the big and successful club they are now. At that time, Widnes and Hull Kingston Rovers were the clubs which always seemed to be winning trophies.

That didn't matter. I was still enthusiastic about cheering on my own team. And I enjoyed the occasion, too, when I travelled with the school party once a year to watch the Challenge Cup Final

Manchester United 'keeper GARY WALSH tells his story.

at Wembley — even if Wigan were not involved.

Until my mid-teens, I played much more rugby than football. It wasn't until a neighbour introduced me to the manager of a boys' club side that I became a goalkeeper.

They'd suddenly found themselves without their regular number one. I was asked to fill in during the emergency, and I've been playing between the posts ever since.

Oddly enough, Manchester United had already watched me playing at centre-forward, but they couldn't have been too impressed, because I didn't hear from them!

When they eventually approached me to sign as a 'keeper, they'd spotted me purely by accident!

I was playing for Wigan Schoolboys against Bolton Schools, and the United scout was there to run the rule over the Bolton goalkeeper.

Fortunately, I must have played better than my

counterpart, because that evening I received a phone call from United, inviting me for trials. The upshot was I joined the club as an apprentice.

Thereafter I made rapid progress at Old Trafford. In fact, the day I made my first-team debut at the age of 18, I realised just how quickly I'd come through the ranks. Just a few months earlier I'd been playing in a Youth Cup Final. Now here I was lining up for a First Division match!

I knew I'd been playing well and I was pleased to have progressed to the reserve team so quickly. I'd even turned out for the first team in a few testimonial matches.

But when manager Alex Ferguson told me the day before the match against Aston Villa that I was playing, I just couldn't believe it.

However, I made a reasonable start, and though I stayed in the team for only four fixtures, I enjoyed a longer run later in the season, and played most of the first half of last term. I was also honoured at international level by playing for the England Under-21's.

Although I was replaced by Chris Turner in the United team shortly before Christmas and had to sit out the next few months, I wasn't too disappointed.

I considered myself very lucky to have gained so much top-level experience so early in my career. Most youngsters of my age, whatever club they are with, are still plugging away at youth or reserve level, hoping eventually to reach senior status.

Besides, at the time, I'd had injury problems which were very worrying. During a club trip to Bermuda, I was on the receiving

Refuse!

end of a kick in the head, which knocked me out. I don't remember a thing about what followed, until waking up in hospital the next morning.

The doctors weren't sure at first of the extent of the problem, but eventually severe bruising was diagnosed and, although I had concussion for a few days, I was assured I had nothing to worry about.

To add to my troubles, however, I went down with a virus shortly afterwards and very quickly lost a stone in weight.

When I was eventually pronounced fit for action, I turned out in a reserve match at Coventry, but even as I took the field, I realised that something was wrong.

I kept feeling dizzy, so Manchester United boss Alex Ferguson suggested I go back into hospital for further brain tests.

Naturally, it was a big weight off my shoulders when I was given the all-clear, along with an explanation that the dizziness was probably caused by my weight loss.

I was allowed to go straight back into light training, but it was several weeks becore I felt one hundred per cent again.

My aim at that time was simply to get myself to a peak again and be ready to challenge for a first-team place at the start of the new season.

Apart from my club ambitions, I also wanted to regain a foothold in the Under-21 England squad.

I knew I'd still have a couple of years left in which I would be qualified to play at that level. But with so many young goalkeepers making their mark in League football, the challenge would be a stiff one.

Whatever happens for the rest of the season, however, I'm still grateful for all that early experience. I know that it will stand me in good stead in my future career.

PROGRAMMES ARE BIG BUSINESS NOW!

● For years, collecting football programmes was a hobby for mainly schoolboy enthusiasts. But now programme collecting is big business. Twenty years ago, there were only a couple of full-time programme dealers in operation. Today that number has risen to almost fifty.

One such dealer is John Garrad, who, in his Midlands Programme Shop, Oxhill Road in Handsworth near Birmingham, stocks every type of programme imaginable.

Another is Steve Earl who owns a shop in Bungay, Suffolk. Steve concentrates on supplying the younger collectors with 1980's material.

Both were schoolboy collectors but their routes into treating programmes as a business were different.

"I began collecting programmes when I was twelve," recalls Steve. "The usual stuff for a beginner — anything colourful and glossy. Soon I started to concentrate on Norwich City programmes because they were the team I supported.

"Then when I was fifteen, my interest fell away a bit and I decided to sell my collection. I had so many enquiries from interested buyers that I thought it might be worthwhile doing some part-time dealing," explains Steve. "This went quite well for five years, so in 1970 I went full-time."

John Garrad, however, went about things differently. He was a collector whilst a director of an engineering firm. In time, though, programmes took priority.

"I couldn't see myself staying in engineering for the rest of my life," says John, "so I gave it up and started up my programme business full time. I was sure there was a market and even though a few folk thought I was off my rocker, I went ahead with it. There were risks obviously, but it was what I wanted to do.

"I ran a mail order operation from home for a time before opening the shop. I've been there fourteen years now," says John, surrounded by 80,000 all-different programmes ranging from pre-war to this week.

John Garrad believes that the

schoolboy collector is being left behind, due to rising prices.

"Five or six years ago if a youngster went to a programme fair and spent £5 he wouldn't be able to carry home his purchases," explains John. "Nowadays he's lucky if he manages to buy ten programmes for that kind of money.

"Recent League programmes can easily be bought at face value, but when it comes to older and big match stuff, prices go up. Cup final and international programmes are very popular collectors' pieces and often in demand, which means the value rises. Pre-war F.A. Cup Final programmes can now be worth up to £85 — depending on condition, of course.

"On my mailing list I have all kinds of people and I try to cater for all their tastes. The schoolboy isn't forgotten though. Current programmes and bargain bundles are also available," John continues.

Steve Earl, on the other hand, caters mainly for the younger collector. He made a decision in the seventies to concentrate on that particular market and deal in more up-to-date programmes. This gives him a stock of over two million!

"I find about 80 per cent of my clients are between eight and twelve years old," explains Steve. "I advertise in their magazines and offer things like an introductory collector's kit including programmes, stickers, pens and pads.

"The most popular programme is Manchester United's. Though I think that if Liverpool were to print more of their programmes, then they would be the most popular," says Steve.

"At present the Anfielders produce relatively few and so they are difficult to get in bulk. This pushes up the price. United, however have a large print, making bulk buying easy.

"As for valuable programmes, I don't stock any as such. I do have a collection of misprints though, where a certain colour is missing or something similar. The thing is that I don't know if these are worth much since I've

never been asked for one!" confesses Steve.

John Garrad, however, is used to highly-priced items. He recalls selling one programme for £300.

"It was a programme for the 1968 World Club Championship played in Buenos Aires between Estudiantes de la Plata and Manchester United. I wasn't even sure a programme had been produced but I managed to track one down via a sailor who had been in port there and been to the game. Finding it gave me a lot of satisfaction," he says.

The business has kept both John and Steve busy for nearly twenty years, and the future looks just as promising.

"Business was good in the seventies following England's World Cup success and the generally healthy state of the

game at that time.

"But then the early 1980's saw a slump. Things are getting better now but it'll take a few years of steady improvement before we get back to the levels of ten or fifteen years ago.

"With a lot of English games being televised abroad there is now a demand for programmes from outside the British Isles. My mailing list includes Australians, Americans and a lot of Scandinavians.

"They are very interested in English soccer and add a new dimension to the market. Along with the upsurge in football popularity again it looks like a rosy future," comments Steve.

And that future seems set to underline that programme collecting is not just for schoolboys, but is an important offshoot of modern day football.

● **John Garrad with two of his most valuable items —
1934 Aston Villa and Chester programmes.**

PUTTING THE BITE ON!

Rangers' goal snatcher ALLY McCOIST gets it in the neck from Aberdeen's ALEX McLEISH.

SHARP

● **CHRIS WADDLE** *Tottenham Hotspur*

● **TERRY WILSON** *Nottingham Forest*

49

HARD KNOCKS

for Norwich City 'keeper BRYAN GUNN

● I've set my sights on a place in Scotland's World Cup squad and if I make it, it'll be thanks to a lamp-post and an electricity power-box!

That was the makeshift goal in the street outside my home when I was a lad. I couldn't add up all the hours I spent throwing myself around between those 'posts' in hard-fought street matches with my friends.

The lamp-post and the electricity box were just the right width apart. And they served a purpose other than just being goalposts. When it got dark, and my dad called me in for bed, I'd hide behind them and pretend I wasn't there! Dad might not have approved at the time, but I'm sure he agrees now that the extra practice was worthwhile.

Those street games were always deadly serious. We'd imagine we were playing World Cup matches for Scotland. Every save was one that took Scotland closer to the trophy.

Now I have the chance to make that dream a reality. In the last year I've managed to win a place in Andy Roxburgh's squad, and I'm desperate to play a part in helping Scotland qualify for the 1990 finals in Italy.

Scotland have won through to the last four finals and I'm confident we can do it again. It's the highlight of any player's career to be involved in the World Cup finals — worth any amount of bruises from diving on the pavement!

It was my dad who got me interested in football. And right from the start I wanted to be a goalkeeper. It was great, diving all over the place, getting muddy. Whenever my friends and I started a game, I always volunteered to go in goal.

In those days Scotland didn't have a great reputation for goalkeepers. Jimmy Greaves built a television career out of taking a rise out of Scottish 'keepers! Now the situation is different. Andy Roxburgh, the Scotland team boss, can call upon as good a bunch of goalkeepers as any international boss.

It's a battle even to get in the squad. A few years ago, just playing regularly in the English First Division would have given me a big advantage when it came to international selection — but not any more.

There are several top 'keepers in the Premier Division north of the border. My ambition to become Scotland's number one gets harder all the time.

I'm in the familiar position of trying to take over from Jim Leighton. It's a situation I faced for six years at Aberdeen at club level. Now my task is to try to push Jim aside in the international team. The job doesn't get any easier.

I joined Aberdeen straight from school at the age of 16. Most players in Scotland have to join a junior club, and play part-time before being picked up by a professional outfit. But I was lucky, and I went almost immediately into Aberdeen's reserve side.

I had high hopes of becoming Aberdeen's first-choice goalkeeper in time, but I reckoned without Jim Leighton. He was so consistent I hardly got a look-in.

Six good years I spent at Pittodrie learning the business from Jim. It was frustrating at times, but it was a good apprenticeship. I went on several European trips and that was fine experience even though I only had a place on the bench.

I did get picked for the Scottish Under-21 side, but I knew that to make real progress I would have to leave Aberdeen to gain regular first-team football.

Norwich City agreed terms for my transfer and it was ironic that my move south was delayed because I was finally required for the Aberdeen first team, due to Jim Leighton being injured.

When he was fit, however, I was allowed to complete the transfer to Norwich and take up a new challenge. And it was quite a challenge because I was replacing a favourite with the Norwich fans, Chris Woods, who had joined Glasgow Rangers.

At the time I was the only Scottish goalkeeper in the First Division. It was said that I was carrying the pressure of having to defend the reputation of Scottish 'keepers in the south and prove the jokes were unjustified.

I didn't see it that way. I felt the standard of goalkeeping in the Premier Division had been rising for a long time. But I was still pleased to be able to show that a Scottish 'keeper could do well in England.

It helped me that Norwich were on a good run. Newly

50

PAID OFF!

● **JIM LEIGHTON (above) — Scotland's man in possession.**

promoted, and without two internationalists, Chris Woods and Dave Watson, who had joined Everton, Norwich surprised everyone by finishing fifth in the table.

It was a great start for me, and helped me to establish myself as a challenger for the international squad. But last season was much tougher. We started badly, and had to work hard to get ourselves out of trouble.

That meant training harder and I must admit that goes against my nature a little. I'm not the world's most dedicated trainer! What I do like is a bit of variety. As a kid you couldn't get me out of goal. But these days in training I like playing in an outfield position.

It's fun to score a few goals in five-a-side training games and as a goalkeeper, trying to score goals gives me a new slant on how best to save them.

I also enjoy playing squash. Not everyone will agree it's a good game for footballers because of the strain on the knees. But I find it's great for improving mobility.

Squash is just one of the ways I like to spend my time away from football. Using my video is another — and not just to watch football. I'm a film buff. At Norwich, and with the Scottish squad, it's my responsibility to organise the videos for the players' relaxation.

The other lads know what to expect — James Bond movies! I have to admit they're my favourite films. I think they're great entertainment — almost as exciting as keeping goal.

My number one 'Bond' is Roger Moore, rather than Sean Connery. But I enjoy them all and I wouldn't mind having a stint at 007 myself! Well, I'm the right size if nothing else.

I've always been tall, and I suppose that's why I was successful in goal as a youngster. Also I've always been agile. My dad was an athlete in the Highland Games, and he passed on his athletic qualities to me.

Running and jumping were his specialities. And speed and good jumping ability are obviously vital for a goalkeeper. Dad was also a useful footballer, and he always encouraged me to play, even if it was only in the street.

I'll always remember those back-street matches. They taught me to take hard knocks — diving on muddy grass is a lot easier than landing on the pavement.

Now I have 18 months to try to establish myself in the Scotland squad as a regular before the World Cup finals.

Over the years I've learned a lot from Jim Leighton. He's a great player to copy. But now I hope to turn that knowledge into good use and eventually take over from Jim as Scotland's number one — thanks to those makeshift goalposts.

● **PETER BEARDSLEY** *Liverpool*

52

● **GRAEME SHARP** *Everton*

PAUL PARKER (Queen's Park Rangers) tells his story

● I've completed my first year in the First Division with Queen's Park Rangers, and in that time my game has improved tremendously, thanks to the coaching staff and to the rude comments from the other players!

I didn't think I was a bad player when I left Fulham to join Q.P.R. but I wasn't as good as I thought. And the other lads at Rangers weren't slow to let me know it!

At Rangers the training is very competitive. All the training drills are done on a competitive basis.

Some clubs give a special shirt to be worn by the player judged the worst in training sessions. Not at Rangers — the players soon let you know if you've had a bad day.

When I first arrived at Rangers I have to admit I took plenty of stick from the others. I knew I just had to work on my game to improve and let someone else become the whipping boy!

I put in plenty of long hours after normal training, doing skill work with coach Peter Shreeve, the former Spurs manager.

Early in the season I was quite nervous in training, but the quick improvement I made paid off. It wasn't long before I was able to give a bit of stick to someone else for a change.

My early problems were really down to a year or two wasted at Fulham. I got into a rut at Craven Cottage and my game stood still for a couple of years.

It was my own fault. As a teenager I signed a very long-term contract tying me to Fulham until 1989, if the club had wanted me to stay.

I should have held out for a

They gave me 'sticl

shorter contract. What happened was that Fulham slipped slowly down the League, sold some of their best players, but priced me out of the market by asking a crazy fee.

Interested clubs were put off by the fee, and being under contract, I couldn't get away. It was very frustrating. My game was standing still while Fulham were struggling to stay in business.

Eventually Rangers stepped in to sign both myself and my best mate Dean Coney for around £450,000, which was less than Fulham originally wanted for me alone.

It was great to be finally given the chance to play in the First Division, but I soon realised I needed to sharpen up physically and mentally.

In the Third Division you can take some liberties and get away with it. In the First, mistakes are punished more quickly. I've had to tighten up my skills and my concentration.

In fact I had to change my whole attitude and the way I played when I stepped up with Rangers. It was very pleasing for me how well things went last season.

When Jim Smith came in for me I couldn't sign quickly enough. It was a three year contract, but in mid-season the manager made me a new offer. He wanted me to re-negotiate my contract and sign a four-year extension. That meant committing myself to Q.P.R. for a further six years.

After my experiences at Fulham, I had to think hard about it — but I was still happy to sign the extended contract. It's a very different situation to the one I was in at Craven Cottage. Financially, I'm much better off. It all adds up to a good deal for me — and a good one I hope for Queen's Park Rangers.

They are an ambitious, go-ahead club. The set-up is geared to success. The sort of plans they have for the stadium — a retractable roof is one idea — show the club wants to be up with the best.

Taking up the artificial pitch and laying a new grass one this year was another step forward. Rangers were the first club to lay a plastic pitch, but now they've

easy to play on the plastic, but it was hard to keep adjusting to grass pitches every other week.

Now Rangers have laid the same type of grass pitch as Fulham had, where the grass grows through a grid that protects the roots and helps drainage. It gives as good a surface as any I've played on.

I think the plastic pitch actually helped me to establish myself in the Rangers defence. As a close-marking defender, I was able to use my natural speed to nip in and take the ball from forwards before they could control it on the hard surface.

But I think I surprised even manager Jim Smith by holding down a place in the centre of the defence, because I'm sure he signed me as a full-back!

In my first few matches in pre-season I played at right-back. But then, two days before our first League match, I played in a practice match in the centre of the defence, alongside Alan McDonald, and with Terry Fenwick as sweeper.

That went so well the boss kept the same line-up for the opening League match at West Ham. Everything fell into place and we won 3-0 to start a great run.

Although I've always enjoyed being a central defender, I'm sure Jim Smith was at first worried about me being caught out because of my size.

as a schoolboy by my local club West Ham because I was too small. But that worked out well in the end. West Ham used to sign up 90 per cent. of the good local boys, but most of them never got anywhere.

I was happy to sign for Fulham, who are a much smaller club. I figured there would be more opportunities for a youngster at a club like Fulham, and that's how it worked out.

I was very happy at Craven Cottage for most of my time there, especially while Malcolm Macdonald was manager. He gave me my first-team chance early one season when Jeff Hopkins was injured, and I was hardly out of the team after that. It was only when the club began to run into financial problems that I felt it was time to leave.

I really enjoyed my first season for Rangers. In football you're up one moment and down the next, so when things are going well you have to make the most of them.

After a two-year break from the international scene it was also nice to be called up for an England B match in Malta, even if I played for only a few minutes.

It would be great for a player like myself, who is too old for the Under-21's, if there were more 'B' team matches.

I'd like to think that I've proved in the last year that I can hold my own at top level. Now I'd

and made me a better player!

moved on.

I was happy to have a year's experience on the plastic surface. It suited me, but I know the older Rangers players were desperate to get rid of it.

To me there were two problems. One was the skin burns you collected every time you fell over. The other was the difficulty in adjusting to a different surface when we played away from Loftus Road. I found it

I'm only five feet seven in my boots, and most defenders are expected to be six-footers. But I've always been able to jump well. I must have natural spring and timing. I find I can match most strikers for high balls.

Some of the Rangers players were a bit astonished when they first saw me in training — they asked if I had specially-sprung boots!

It's ironic that I was rejected

like to step up to the England squad.

The 1990 World Cup finals are the target I'm aiming at, but I'm not building my hopes too high. I have to concentrate on playing consistently well for Q.P.R., and hope, as a bonus, to earn selection for the England squad

That would make all the hard work and all the tongue lashings well worthwhile.

● **BRIAN McCLAIR** *Manchester United*

● **TONY DORIGO** *Chelsea*

PRICELESS!

TALENT SPOTTERS WITH THE MIDAS TOUCH

⬤ **January 30th, 1988 may not be the most memorable date in the minds of Manchester City fans. But it was still a proud day in the club's history.**

Nothing momentous you might think about an FA Cup fourth round 1-1 draw with Blackpool on that date.

However, compare City's squad at Bloomfield Road that afternoon with the line-up for the Maine Road side's FA Youth Cup Final victory over Manchester United less than two years earlier and you'll find seven of the names are the same!

The other four members of that successful 'kids' team have left the club. But the remaining players appeared together in the first team for the first time against Blackpool.

Andy Hinchcliffe, Paul Lake, Steve Redmond, David White, Paul Moulden Ian Brightwell and Ian Scott were the youngsters — not one of them over 20 at the time — who graduated from that youth side to the seniors.

The men who made the achievement possible weren't at the seaside that day to witness their handiwork. They were elsewhere — on school playing fields and public parks continuing the never-ending search for more talent.

Former Maine Road star from the fifties, Ken Barnes, heads the City team of talent spotters.

His colleagues run their eyes over likely lads and it's Barnes' job to act on their judgment and secure the promising youngsters for the club.

The early eighties were a golden period for Barnes and his scouts. That's

when those seven on duty at Blackpool began springing up in junior football.

When Barnes signed up these boys just out of primary school he was securing a future pot of gold for City. Envious clubs have waved tempting cheques under the noses of City chairman Peter Swales and his management team of Mel Machin and Jimmy Frizzell.

They refused all offers and are sitting on a potential income of over £3 million if they decided to unload all of their young stars.

That's some profit on boys who cost the club absolutely nothing and a huge testimony to the ability of Ken Barnes and his staff to spot promising material at such a tender age.

Once a prospect is spotted he's invited to Maine Road for trials during school holidays. If he measures up, he will then progress through City's nursery teams Allestock, Blue Stars and Midas.

The 'magnificent seven' all trod a similar route. Most have played together since they were only 12 years old.

Barnes declares modestly, "You don't have to be someone special to recognise talent when it confronts you. And it was clear these lads had it.

"Paul Lake, for instance, who is now an England Under-21 player, was obviously something special even when he was 12.

"He has since grown into a big, strong lad but when I was first notified about him he was small and frail. But despite his size he had plenty of ability. He was doing stuff you rarely see in a youngster. He was one for the book

straightaway.

"Another sure bet was Steve Redmond. But, although he now operates as a defender, it was as a striker that he first came to my attention," explains Barnes.

"He was a prolific goalscorer on his native Merseyside. Liverpool, Everton and other top clubs were showing interest, so we brought him to Maine Road with his parents and they liked the way we looked after the young lads.

"We don't make any rash promises to them. Most mums and dads can spot super-salesmanship when they see it. We were happy to secure Steve because he was obvious quality.

"I look for little things in their game at that early age which are giveaway signs that they have what it takes," says Ken Barnes.

"Boys of that age are mainly chasing after the ball all the time and kicking and rushing. Steve Redmond had an awareness and composure that you don't often see in a youngster."

Andy Hinchcliffe is arguably the most sought after of City's batch of starlets. Manchester United and Rangers showed strong interest last season and Spurs were just waiting for the nod from Maine Road and a cheque would have been in the post with the ink still wet!

Like Redmond, Hinchcliffe, now a left back, was spotted as a forward.

"He was operating as an outside-left for Trafford Boys," explains Ken Barnes. "But he didn't have enough craft or guile to make it on the wing.

"However, his attitude, pace and control were spot on. He also had a

MIDAS (11/12 years old) BACK ROW — LEFT TO RIGHT 2. Andy Hinchcliffe 6. David White 7. Steve Redmond 8. Ian Brightwell.

MIDAS 8-A-SIDE (13/14 years old) BACK ROW — LEFT TO RIGHT 1. Paul Lake 3. David White 4. Andy Hinchcliffe.
FRONT ROW 1. Ian Brightwell 2. Ian Scott.

lovely left foot. With so many naturally right-footed lads around, those who can use their left, and especially one as good as Andy's, are a rarity. I had no hesitation recommending him, but I knew he wouldn't make it on the wing."

One youngster who did was David White. The strapping six-footer is another who has graduated to international honours for England at Under-21 level. But it was White's well built frame that put a question mark over him in Ken Barnes' mind.

"You couldn't overlook David at that age because he was bigger than most of the kids around him," Ken recalls. "However, I'm always wary of players like that because it can often be the case that size alone gets them through. You wonder whether they will be as effective when everyone else catches up on them.

"But David wasn't just a big lad. He had ability, pace and packed a terrific punch in his shots. In my mind I could always see a place for him in football," enthuses Ken.

It isn't always size or ability that edges the vote in favour of a promising youngster. Take the case of midfielder Ian Brightwell.

"Ian didn't come over as anything exceptional when he was first brought to our notice," Barnes explains.

"But I liked his determination. I knew he had a good family pedigree with his mother and father being former Olympic medal-winning athletes Robbie Brightwell and Ann Packer.

"He'd obviously inherited his parents' stamina. But it was his excellent attitude to the game that made him worth an apprenticeship."

Few of the best boys can be kept away from the attention of other club scouts. There was certainly no way Paul Moulden's ability was going to be a hush-hush affair. He earned himself a place in the Guinness Book of Records for his goalscoring!

Two hundred and eighty-nine goals in one 40-game season for Bolton Lads Club ensured Moulden's place in the famous book and in the note-pads of many talent-spotters.

Barnes goes on, "From the first time I saw him I could see he had exactly what it takes to be a goalscorer. Basically he knew where the goals were and invariably put the ball there!

"Thankfully he liked what he saw at Maine Road and agreed to sign for us."

Whilst the other six of the FA Youth Cup-winning side were snatched up, one player, Ian Scott, initially escaped Manchester City's clutches.

"Ian had signed for another League club. Apparently he agreed to the first one that approached him," recalls Ken.

"He soon realised he had made a mistake and I learned that Ian had asked to have his contract cancelled.

"I had seen him play and liked the way he passed a ball. He had a footballing vision that was hard to find in 14-year-olds."

Ken Barnes' seal of approval continues to secure the top boys for Manchester City. And the network of scouts employed by the club is arguably even more envied than the talent it eventually produces.

Pricing the likes of Andy Hinchcliffe and Paul Lake is the easy bit. Putting a figure on the team who search them out is impossible.

● **PAUL MOULDEN — a place in the record books.**

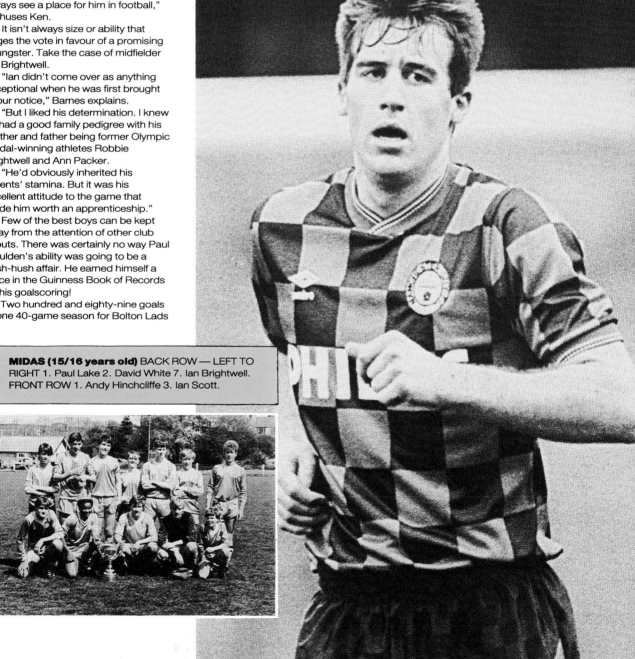

MIDAS (15/16 years old) BACK ROW — LEFT TO RIGHT 1. Paul Lake 2. David White 7. Ian Brightwell. FRONT ROW 1. Andy Hinchcliffe 3. Ian Scott.

● **FRANZ CARR** *Nottingham Forest*

The Race is On

Arsenal's **TONY ADAMS** stretches every muscle to cope with the pace and power of Liverpool's explosive **JOHN BARNES**.

IN THE HOT SEAT!

Everton's Gary Stevens faces the questions – and gives his answers.

Was there ever a stage when you thought you wouldn't make it as a professional?

I think all apprentices have their doubts from time to time. For my part, I could have stayed on at school and picked up some qualifications but I chose football instead. There are bound to be times when you wonder if you have made the right decision.

I've seen a lot of good friends drop out of football over the years. That's one of the reasons I've always set so much store on physical fitness — to give me the best possible chance of making the grade.

Were you always a right-back?

No. When I first signed for Everton I was a right-winger. From there I moved to the left side of midfield. It was only when present Everton manager Colin Harvey was put in charge of the reserve side that I was converted to the number two shirt.

How much has your physical fitness helped your career?

It was vital early on when I was competing for a place in the Everton first team against Brian Borrows, who is now at Coventry.

It was very close between us. The manager at the time, Howard Kendall, told me I was getting the nod because I was a bit stronger and quicker than Brian and that is very important when it comes to recovering if you are beaten or caught out of position.

Do you still work hard on your fitness?

I do all the training the other lads do but there are occasions when I'll stay behind in the afternoon and do a bit extra if I feel it's needed.

I know my fitness is my major asset. I don't have the silky skills of team-mates such as Trevor Steven or Kevin Sheedy.

Achieving a physical peak might just be gained by making that extra run in a game of five-a-sides. That enables you to produce a bit extra in a match situation when the need arises.

You established yourself in the senior side just at the time Everton began to mount a major revival. Coincidence?

I'd known a couple of the struggling years when we weren't in the running for silverware. At that stage I was in and out of the side.

I really tied down a first-team place during the 1983-84 season, which was the year the present run of success began. I suppose we all played a part in that and it was certainly the right time to come into the side.

The first big game I played in was the all-Merseyside 1983-84 Milk Cup Final. We lost in the replay, but after that game we put together a run which took us back to Wembley to win the FA Cup against Watford.

That sequence gave us the impetus for what was to follow — two League Championships, the European Cup Winners' Cup and two more FA Cup Finals.

Were you surprised to progress so quickly to the England squad?

I made my England debut at the end of the 1984-85 season and I think I benefited from the fact there was so much public pressure on Bobby Robson to select Everton players because the team had done so well.

We won the League and the European Cup-Winners' Cup without anyone making the breakthrough. But by the finish of that campaign, Peter Reid, Trevor Steven, Paul Bracewell, and myself had been 'capped'.

I made my debut against Italy in a tournament in Mexico which was to acclimatise us for the World Cup Finals the following year.

Then I played against West Germany in the same competition, so my first cap has the names of two of the greatest football nations embroidered on it. It's something I'll treasure forever.

That debut was made in fairly difficult circumstances, wasn't it?

Yes, in the sense that we were up against Italy just a few days after the Heysel Stadium disaster. A lot of Italian fans had been killed in the trouble before the European Cup Final between Juventus and Liverpool.

But to some degree we were sheltered from the worst of it because we were in Mexico. We didn't sense any hostility, though we obviously knew it was an important match to be involved in.

From a personal point of view the game went well, though I gave away a penalty. Not the way I'd have wanted to start my England career, but it was such a bad refereeing decision that I didn't lose any sleep about it.

You didn't have the usual international background, did you?

No. Though I'd had one previous non-playing call-up, it wasn't until after the 1984 Cup Final that I made my Under-21 debut, the last match for which I was qualified to play.

It was the second leg of the final of the UEFA Under-21 tournament — against Spain at Bramall Lane. I didn't get into the action until three minutes from the end when manager Dave Sexton sent me on as a substitute simply to make sure I won a cap.

I took a throw-in and collected a medal! But that summed up the way things were going for me at that point. Everything seemed to fall my way.

Is the presence of team-mate Trevor Steven in the England squad a big help to you?

Trevor and I are very good friends and room together when we're away on international duty. But though we each have over twenty caps, we haven't played together all that often.

But when we are on the field together it

is a big help to have him in front of me. We have a good understanding at club level and try to transfer that to the England side.

You have had plenty of career highlights — which stands out as the best?

You're right, there have been many moments to remember. Winning the FA Cup, the Championship, and taking home the European Cup-Winners' Cup take some beating.

But though all those occasions ended with us lifting a trophy, the day which stands out most of all was one when we didn't actually have anything tangible to show for it.

That highlight came in the semi-final of that Cup-Winners' Cup competition when we came back from a goal down at Goodison to beat Bayern Munich 3-1 and secure a spot in the final against Rapid Vienna in Rotterdam.

It was a magnificent night with a tremendous atmosphere. I've never been involved in anything quite like it before or since.

What has been the worst moment of your career?

No doubt about that one! Being taken off in the 1986 FA Cup Final against Liverpool after being at fault for their equalising goal.

I gave the ball away out on the right touchline and Jan Molby set up Ian Rush for a goal which put them back into the game. I stayed on for another 15 minutes, during which time the Anfielders took the lead, then Howard Kendall replaced me with Adrian Heath.

It didn't do much good because we were exposed in defence after that and ended up losing 3-1.

I felt like walking straight to the dressing-room after my number had been held up. To be substituted at Wembley is a terrible moment.

I made myself take a seat on the bench and watch the rest of the game. But it wasn't easy, I can tell you!

There was also a very sad incident in your career, wasn't there?

Yes, the one which saw Liverpool left-back Jim Beglin break his leg when I tackled him during a Littlewoods Cup-tie in 1987.

The whole country must have seen the incident on TV. I've watched videos of it since and still don't know how such a horrific thing could have happened.

There was no malice in my challenge and at first I didn't even believe I'd hurt Jim. It was a 50-50 ball and it's frightening to realise something so simple could put a player out of the game for over a year.

I took a bit of blame from the Liverpool camp at the time it happened, but they were quick to apologise afterwards. The fans gave me a bit of stick in the first couple of 'derbies' after that, but, again, it blew over.

● **ALLY McCOIST** *Rangers*

65

Football abounds with myths and legends. The best known surround the players, of course. Tales of great matches, magnificent goals and unforgettable characters pepper the memories of all fans.

But there are other stories passed down from generation to generation which centre on the places the game is played in . . . the grounds.

Practically every League club has some tale or other about their home patch. Sometimes every word is perfectly true. On other occasions the yarn has been embellished in its re-telling, but always there is substance to the tales.

So sit back, dim the lights and prepare to suspend your imagination. You are about to enter football's twilight zone . . .

Did you know, for instance, that there's a curse on Birmingham City's St Andrew's ground?

It was visited on the club eighty years ago when gypsies were turfed off the land to make room for the ground's construction.

The head gypsy declared that the club would never be successful — and as City have never won a major trophy, who knows if the power of the spell has hung over the stadium for these years?

Certainly former manager Ron Saunders took it seriously. A priest, a rabbi, a Church of England minister and a faith healer were invited to the ground a few years ago to exorcise the curse.

Gold crosses were placed on the floodlights and a crucifix hung in the dressing-room corridor. The players painted the soles of their boots red because it is believed that colour wards off evil!

In the months that followed, City were relegated to Division Two, dumped out of the FA Cup by non-League Altrincham and Saunders was sacked from the manager's job!

At Oldham Athletic's Boundary Park there is reputed to be a ghost. Named Fred, he is said to walk the terraces where he stood as a fan until his death in the early 1960's.

And have you ever wondered why Liverpool enjoy attacking the Spion Kop end of the ground when they play at Anfield?

Statistics show around three-quarters of the team's total number of home goals are scored in front of that famous bank of massed support.

Former manager Bob Paisley reckons that the huge overhanging roof, plus the turbulence caused by the noise of the crowd, actually sucks the ball towards the net at that end.

Incidentally, have you ever noticed a flag pole just behind the Kop where it joins the Kemlyn Road stand?

Originally this was the mast

THEY COULDN'T because of a dead

from the Great Eastern, one of the world's first iron ships, which was broken up in Liverpool docks in 1888.

Forty years later the mast was floated across the Mersey and dragged to Anfield by a team of horses.

Unexpected items are to be found at many grounds ... like the five-legged chair in the boardroom at Highbury.

It was apparently made for a former director who suffered from gout. He was in the habit of rising suddenly to his feet in pain and the extra leg was to prevent his chair being knocked over.

London neighbours Chelsea are credited with being the first club to employ ball-boys.

Back in 1906, the manager, John Tait Robertson, decided it would be a good idea to exploit the impressive physique of his goalkeeper, Willie Foulke.

Foulke was 6 ft. 3 in. tall and weighed in at over 20 stone. Robertson placed two small

● RON SAUNDERS

● BOB PAISLEY

boys behind Foulke's goal to emphasise his enormous frame in the hope of putting off opposing strikers.

Mind you, it was a miracle that football was ever played at Stamford Bridge at all. The fate of the ground rested on the bite of a dog!

Just after the turn of the century, owner Gus Mears didn't think the site viable for football and was about to sell it off to the Great Western Railway as a coal dumping yard.

His friend, Frederick Parker, opposed the idea, but Mears mistrusted his judgment until the day Mears' dog bit Parker on the leg.

Parker reacted in such a cool, level-headed manner that Mears decided that here was a man whose opinion should be respected. He decided to develop the ground for football.

At that time, Stamford Bridge was used for Cup Finals. Another ground which got in on that particular act was Burnden Park,

home of Bolton Wanderers.

In 1901 the club hosted the replay of the Tottenham v. Sheffield United Final. The first match at Crystal Palace had attracted a crowd of nearly 115,000 and the merchants of the Lancashire town rubbed their hands at the prospect of making a financial killing from the sale of food to the hungry thousands.

But because of re-development work at the local railway station, many of the fans couldn't travel. Only 20,000 turned up and huge mountains of food were wasted. The day became known in the town as 'Pie Saturday.'

Fans in South Wales will know that there is a concrete slab at Swansea's Vetch Field ground inscribed with the name of former Wales, Leeds and Juventus star John Charles.

Charles himself etched his name in the stone — actually mis-spelling his surname before correcting it — when he was a young supporter of the club. He stood on it to give him a better view of the game.

Finally, Bury were once prevented from scoring by a dead budgie. The bird was the pet of a fanatical supporter who, when the budgie died, asked for permission to bury it in one goalmouth at Gigg Lane.

Problem was, that no matter how they tried, the home team just couldn't score at that end of the pitch! The bird had to be located and removed before the goals started to flow again!

CORE — budgie

— ONLY ONE OF MANY FASCINATING STORIES FROM THE FOOTBALL GROUNDS

IT'S A TOUGH GAME!

Rain soaked, mud splattered, Middlesbrough's TONY MOWBRAY shows that being a professional footballer is not a bed of roses!

● **TONY ADAMS** *Arsenal*

Hammer blo

1. Liverpool 'keeper Bruce Grobbelaar leaves his goal to meet a cross into the penalty box.

2. Hampered by friend and foe, Bruce fails to make a clean catch.

3. The ball breaks to Everton striker Wayne Clarke — who hits the back of the net.

or record hunting reds !

It's the Anfielders' thirtieth League game of the season. Unbeaten in the previous twenty-nine, they only need to avoid defeat to beat Leeds United's long-standing record of twenty-nine successive League matches without defeat. But one moment of disaster was enough to rob the Reds of their place in the history books.

4. Jubilation for the Everton players — but bitter disappointment for Bruce Grobbelaar and his team-mates.

CLOSE ENCOUNTER

Everton's goal hungry GRAEME SHARP (left) battles to escape the clutches of Coventry's BRIAN KILCLINE.

● **KEITH STEVENS** *Millwall*

SIDELINES

The off-beat side of Football

IN THE BAG

TRAVEL TROUBLE

LEIGHTON JAMES
(Burnley)

I remember one harrowing journey during m[...] time with Bury. It was early on in the 1984-85 season and we had to make the long haul to Devon to play Exeter City.

We set off from Gigg Lane early one Saturd[...] morning in good spirits. We had started the campaign well and were unbeaten in the Leagu[...] We were quite unprepared for what lay ahead o[...] us on the motorway.

Our team coach got caught up in a most horrendous traffic jam, in a lot of holiday traffic you're going to the Devon or Cornwall holiday spots then Exeter just happens to be one of the[...] places en-route that most traffic goes through.

When travelling to away games we would usually take some sandwiches with us to eat on the return trip. This meant that we didn't have t[...] stop on the way home, so speeding up our retu[...] If it was a long journey we would, instead, stop somewhere on the way to the game for lunch.

On this occasion, there was no time for a lunch stop as it looked likely we would be late f[...] kick-off. So, we ate our after-match sandwiche[...] as a pre-match meal!

We arrived at the ground just in time to get changed and take the field. You would imagine that a trip like that would have an adverse effec[...] but it worked out just the opposite. We played Exeter off the park and took home three points [...] virtue of a 2-0 win.

Even if that wasn't the biggest shock of the da[...] though. The girl in a local chip shop got that on[...] our way back to Bury when we stopped the coa[...] and ordered fifteen portions of fish and chips. I[...] don't think they did us any harm either. We did [...] on to win promotion to the Third Division after a[...]

RON FUTCHER
(Bradford City)

I had a terrifying experience while playing for Minnesota Kicks in the North American Soccer League.

We were setting off for a match in Seattle when the plane developed engine trouble.

The trouble was, the fault did not show itself until we were well down the runway and about to take off.

We were at full speed and only a couple of seconds from leaving the ground when the pilot slammed on the brakes and we went skidding down the runway.

It was nerve-shattering, especially as it was some moments before we knew exactly what was happening. Then we had a two-hour wait while the problem was put right before a nerve-wracking but successful second attempt at taking off.

Because the teams in the NASL were so widespread we had to travel by plane to nearly all our away matches. The most tedious trip of all was when we were going to Chicago.

The airport there is so busy that, even after seeing the city below us, we'd have to circle for an hour as we awaited clearance to land.

All around, we could see other planes caught up in the traffic jam, and occasionally we'd change places with another plane as we queued up for our turn.

Most goal-keepers carry a bag with spare gloves, caps and other useful items. But there are some who take along something special . . .

ANDY RHODES
(Oldham Athletic)

I ought to be the world's luckiest goalkeeper with the amount of charms I carry in my glove bag.

Firstly there are my girlfriend's beads, which she gave me for luck. Then there are the "keys to the door" I received when I became twenty one.

Both my parents and my girlfriend sent me one of the traditional silver keys so I placed them alongside the beads in my bag. All three items are there to give me that little bit of luck that might just turn a game.

CHRIS PEARCE
(Burnley)

Six Christmases ago whilst I was with Rochdale, someone threw me a small plastic red robin from the crowd. I had a good game that day so I decided to keep it amongst my gloves and cap in the goal.

That was added to last season at the time of the 'Comic Relief' appeal. We were playing at Swansea when a Burnley supporter threw me a red nose. There was no clowning around on my part, however. I had another good game, keeping a clean sheet, and the nose and the robin have been with me ever since.

NIGEL SPACKMAN
Liverpool

I began my career at Bournemouth when comedian Jim Davidson was a director at Dean Court. Obviously he watched most of our games and was close to the players.

He gave me a lot of tickets for his shows down south. We became friends and have followed each others careers ever since.

Many top players have friends outside the game. Here are just some who are friends of the famous.

KEVIN MACDONALD
Liverpool

Gary Lineker was a team-mate of mine at Leicester City and he was a very keen snooker fan. Through him all the players at Filbert Street were invited to become members of Willie Thorne's club in the area.

I'm not a very good snooker player but I had a few frames with Willie on occasions.

I've kept a close eye on his matches and see him whenever I return to Leicester.

COLIN HENDRY
Blackburn Rovers

I first got to know 'Fish', lead singer of Marillion when he was a community programme worker in my home town Keith, in Scotland. He used to organise five-a-side games each Friday evening and I frequently went along to join in.

He knew me only as one of the crowd but when the band started doing gigs I'd go and watch. Eventually they became more successful, they played further afield and we lost touch a little.

Fish is aware of my successes here though through a friend of mine in the record business. Hopefully this will lead to us meeting up again soon for a good old chinwag.

PETER BEARDSLEY
Liverpool

When I was at Newcastle United with Kevin Keegan and Terry McDermott they were very keen horse-racing fans.

Through them I became very friendly with jockey Neale Doughty. I had a flutter on him when he rode Hello Dandy in the Grand National in 1984 and he won!

Oddly enough, only two players in the Newcastle camp didn't have money on Neale — his best mates Keegan and McDermott!

We've remained friends since and I'm always trying to see Neale race whenever I'm free of my football commitments.

PAUL SHANE

GLYNN SNODIN
Leeds Utd.

I got to know Paul Shane well when he worked down the coal mines with my father near Rotherham. Paul was always an entertainer and started off by filling in for artists who failed to turn up at the miners' social clubs. He would get up, tell a few jokes and sing a bit, too.

Eventually his appearances became more regular and we would often go and see him perform. My brother Ian (Ian Snodin — Everton) and I got to know him even better when we visited our grandma in Dalton as Paul lives just a couple of doors down the road from her.

It was great to see Paul do well on "Hi-de-Hi" and we were delighted for him when he got the break. One minute it was a thirty-second part on "Coronation Street", then the star of "Maplins Holiday Camp". It couldn't have happened to a nicer bloke.

PERRY SUCKLING
(Crystal Palace)

On the morning of my last birthday I received a birthday card from a young fan. Inside was taped a pound coin.

I was going through a difficult patch with Manchester City at that time and found this very touching. Such a nice gesture, in fact, that I decided to keep the coin as a good luck charm even after I moved from Maine Road to join Crystal Palace.

Now I never fail to take it out on to the pitch amongst my cap and gloves.

SCOTT BARRETT
(Stoke City)

I don't really know why but I keep a bird's feather in my glove bag!

I came across the feather during my time with Wolves. Walking in a local park I saw it lying on the ground. For some reason I picked it up and took it home, then put it in amongst my gloves.

Although I'm no real bird expert I think it's a magpie's feather. One thing I am sure about, however, is that for the time being at least I'm going to keep it. Now I look on it as my lucky charm.

● ALAN McDONALD *Queen's Park Rangers*

LAST *GASP* GARY

Tottenham Hotspur defender GARY MABBUTT makes a desperate effort to halt the progress of Arsenal's ALAN SMITH.

KEEP SMILING!

Smile — you're playing for Brian Clough! Not actually an instruction handed out to players at Nottingham Forest, but it isn't far from the mark.

Our manager has always had a reputation for turning out teams which rarely fall foul of referees. The boss insists that if you commit an offence on the park, you pick up your opponent and say you're sorry. It doesn't hurt to be pleasant rather than aggressive if ever a ref calls you over.

I've always been a smiler. Maybe that is what has kept my bookings to a minimum and stopped me from picking up any suspensions. If I've done something wrong I apologise and try to be as courteous as possible.

I'm not a naturally aggressive character in any case. But at six feet four inches and fourteen stone, you would think there could be times when my very size might land me in bother. When you're built like I am, sometimes you only have to nudge a smaller opponent for him to fall over. Yet officials seem to make allowances for that.

I suppose you would have to class me as something of a gentle giant. Certainly I believe people thought of me in that way at my first club, Leyton Orient. And I guess the same applies at Forest.

But despite my size, I've always thought of myself as reasonably nimble. I'm quite comfortable with the ball at my feet. I'm not the kind of centre-half whose only thought is to hoof it upfield.

Brian Clough likes me to concentrate on defensive duties first and foremost. But if the occasion arises, he has no objection to me trying something a little more ambitious.

The fact that I'm not perhaps as clumsy looking as some

That's the way to play for Nottingham Forest's COLIN FOSTER.

players of my size, could stem from the practice I put in with a tennis ball when I was about 14 or 15.

I always wanted to make a career in the game and I realised that using a smaller-than-average size ball would probably help my footwork.

Mind you, there was one person in the Foster household who wasn't too keen on my becoming a footballer — my mum.

She considered it a job that didn't have much security attached to it. She would have preferred it if I'd become a policeman!

She has seen me play only once or twice. And when I go home to London, football is

● BRIAN CLOUGH

rarely a talking point when she is around. In fact, there are times when if I want to watch a game on TV, I have to video it.

All this, however, does have the effect of keeping my feet firmly on the ground. With my mum around, there's no chance of me running away with the idea that I'm some sort of star!

My dad is the exact opposite. He's a football fanatic. He travels on the coach run by the London Branch of the Forest Supporters Club, to watch every game I play.

But when it comes to making sure players keep their feet planted firmly on the deck, there is, of course, none better at that than Mr Clough himself.

For instance, during those weeks when half the players at the club are away on duty for various international squads, the 'leftovers', as we call ourselves, are usually pressed into service for the Forest reserve team.

I had an early experience of the manager's ways. I was an Orient player at the time with getting on for 200 first team games behind me. It had been arranged that I come up to Nottingham for a trial with a view to eventually signing.

And a trial it certainly was! I turned out for the Forest 'A' team on a park pitch at half past ten on a Saturday morning!

My transfer eventually went through, fulfilling a promise my manager at Brisbane Road had made to me on the day he put the block on a possible transfer to Wimbledon.

Frank Clark, the Orient boss, was a player under Brian Clough at Forest and the two are still great friends.

When Wimbledon made a bid for me during the season they were promoted to the First Division, Frank turned it down and told me he would sort out something better for me.

When it turned out to be Forest, I couldn't wait to sign. I played the back end of the '86-

'87 campaign then had the whole of last season in the team.

Even now, as I'm still relatively new to the top level, I consider myself "on trial." I'm learning all the time. Not least the fact that your concentration has to be total in the First Division.

I learned my lessons last season. Particularly in a Littlewoods Cup-tie against Manchester City at Maine Road. My concentration let me down and I was at fault for two goals which cost us a place in the next round.

Then I saw the number five board being held up on the touchline. The manager wanted me off because of the errors.

I must admit I was shocked. I had made mistakes at Orient and not been substituted. In fact, for tactical reasons, it is very unusual to see any centre-half being dragged off.

The boss didn't say a word afterwards. And that made it worse. The whole incident really woke me up and made me determined it would never happen again.

My defensive partner Des Walker has been brilliant at helping me. Though I'm older, he's much more experienced at top level than I am and whenever my concentration has looked like slipping, Des has been there talking, putting me on the right track again.

We all have to set our minds to the job here. We know Brian Clough wouldn't hesitate to replace any of us with a 17-year-old unknown if he thought it was best for the club.

Playing in the First Division is everything I imagined it would be. I just hope I can continue to make progress and improve as a top-flight player.

● **GORDON DURIE** *Chelsea*

● **BILLY THOMSON** *Dundee United*

There is an old, sad song containing the lines... "I'm gonna sit right down and write myself a letter, and make believe it came from you!"

Well, just over three years ago I didn't exactly sit down and write to myself. But I did send letters to every football club in the English First and Second Divisions and all the Premier Division outfits in Scotland. Fifty-six in all!

I'd spent five months sitting on the sidelines, after failing to agree a new contract with Albion Rovers, and that was my way of making one last, desperate bid to save my career.

I'd finished the previous season as Scotland's leading marksman with 31 goals. But still Albion Rovers weren't prepared to give me the kind of contract I was after. What's more, according to them, no other club was interested in me.

The future looked decidedly bleak. I was even banned from taking any active part at the club. And I knew the part-time job I held as a gardener was only short-term. The dole queue was staring me in the face.

Even as I sat and wrote those letters in search of a fresh start, I had the feeling it was a lost cause. It really was a last ditch effort as far as I was concerned.

I received 18 replies from clubs south of the border. Just one arrived from a Scottish club — Hearts.

It was, however, a 'phone call and not a letter that was to set me up for the most amazing three years I'll ever experience in football.

That call came within two days of dropping my letters in the post-box. Willie Maddren, then boss of Middlesbrough, was the bloke on the line. And he was offering me a two-week trial.

Because Willie was the first manager to make contact, I felt duty bound to accept his offer. Another couple of weeks and the fairytale was made complete when I signed a full-time contract with the Teesside club.

Nothing has happened since to make me regret that decision. Not even the fact that barely eight months later I was left wondering whether I'd jumped out of the frying pan straight into the fire.

By then Middlesbrough had not only been relegated from the Second Division, but the club was locked and shuttered as the liquidators threatened to close the club down.

Those were grim summer days. Come pre-season we had to change in our cars and train anywhere we could find under new manager Bruce Rioch.

At one stage things became so bad that we went six weeks without being paid. And all we could do during that time was simply to hope that some financial miracle would arrive to save the club . . . and our jobs.

In fact, it was only on the very eve of the following season, that the club, after a lot of tremendously hard work behind the scenes, was finally given the all clear to carry on.

But, even then, it wasn't in time to let us kick off the new campaign on our own pitch. Opening day found us in action against Port Vale at the Victoria Ground home of neighbouring Hartlepool.

What has happened since that day now rates as one of the most remarkable come-back stories the game has ever produced.

From the brink of disaster, we won promotion back to Division Two that same season and last term we added yet another chapter to one of the game's greatest fairy-tales by reaching the First Division.

The 40-odd goals I popped in during that amazing recovery also made me very grateful that I'd become a man of 'letters' those surprisingly brief three years before!

Letters Saved Me From The Scrapheap!

Middlesbrough's BERNIE SLAVEN explains why.

● **ROBERT FLECK** *Norwich City*

● **COLIN CLARKE** *Southampton*

BATTLE of the BIG MEN!

Everton's DAVE WATSON (left) fights to hold off the challenge of LEE CHAPMAN (Sheffield Wednesday).

● **MEL STERLAND** *Sheffield Wednesday*

HOW TO BE A BOSS

Peter Withe gives the low-down on the school for the football managers of the future.

● In Peter Withe's trophy-case lying beside League Championship and European Cup-Winners' medals and England caps, is a piece of paper which means as much to him as any of his more 'traditional' honours.

It is a certificate denoting that the much-travelled striker has successfully completed the Management Course run by the football authorities at a college in St Helens on Merseyside.

It's a two-week programme designed to teach players the basics of club management.

Peter attended the course during the summer of 1987. Here he gives his account of how the footballers of today are sent back to school to become the managers of tomorrow.

The course is a tough one, with long hours and loads of writing. It is just like being back at school. But it's very, very interesting.

The object is to give players a grounding in the running of a football club. Every aspect from the commercial side to the work of a physiotherapist is covered. Guest lecturers are brought in to talk to the class during the two weeks.

My group — which consisted of twenty-four players, the maximum the course can cater for each summer — had talks from League Secretary Graham Kelly, President Philip Carter, Oldham Athletic chairman Ian Stott, and managers such as Ian Greaves (Mansfield), John McGrath (Preston) and Mick Mills of Stoke.

Mick had attended the 'school' in a previous year. He had landed a boss's job and had come back to tell us what help the course had been.

The main object of the course is to teach business management. Most of the rules which apply to running a commercial company also apply to a League football club.

You learn about computers, for instance. About the work of people within a club whom players don't usually have close contact with — the secretary, the chairman, the board of directors, and the medical and commercial staff.

Most of all, you are told how a manager's job fits in with the other roles within the club.

To help with this the group is presented with a fictitious football team. Ours was Frackleton Town. And over the two weeks we acted out various jobs within that club.

For instance, one of us would have to apply for the manager's job. The others would take on the parts of the chairman and directors at the interview. This was videoed and then replayed, with the lecturers pointing out where mistakes were made.

I probably worked harder during that fortnight than at any time in my football career. There was just one day off — Sunday — and the lessons lasted from nine in the morning until nine at night.

There were breaks for meals, but as study and preparation work were often required after the daily lectures were over, you were kept busy almost every minute.

But the accommodation and hospitality at the college were excellent. And by the time we'd finished, all the players were close friends. We still keep in touch.

There were players such as Paul Mariner, Sam Allardyce, Barry Powell, Ian Atkins and Paul Jones in the class. All of us went with an eye to one day becoming a boss — but I don't know if everyone still fancies it now they know the work and effort it entails!

It certainly opened my eyes. As a player you see only one aspect of a manager's problems. Now I appreciate what he and everyone else at a club has to put up with.

But it didn't put me off my desire to be a successful manager. The course was very valuable experience and I'd recommend it to anybody.

At the end you are given the certificate which says you have successfully completed the course. That certificate is something I, for one, am very proud of.

● **KENNY WHARTON** *Newcastle United*

● **GLYN HODGES** *Wimbledon*

89

● **DAVID PHILLIPS** *Coventry City*

● **STEVE NICOL** *Liverpool*

● **PAUL ALLEN** *Tottenham Hotspur*

LATE STARTER – BUT I'LL MAKE THE MOST OF IT!

● I was born in the same place as Ian Rush — St Asaph in North Wales. Rushie is just seven months older than me so we played together in several school teams.

I didn't dream that Ian and I would both play for our country together — but that's exactly what happened last season when I made my debut for Wales against Yugoslavia in Swansea.

What made that even more surprising was that I never expected to become a professional footballer at all.

When I left school I went to Liverpool University, where I studied for a degree in chemistry. At the same time I was also playing for Rhyl in the Northern Premier League. I was quite happy with that situation and I hadn't really considered playing football at a higher level.

I passed my degree and I decided to stay on at university to do a PhD in Metallurgy. It was soon after that Wrexham offered me the chance to play League football. I decided to take the chance and become a professional footballer at the age of 22.

I had some great times with Wrexham and I suppose the highlights really came in my first season. The club qualified for the European Cup-Winners' Cup and in the first round we played Porto from Portugal, a team that was to win the European Cup three years later.

The first leg was at home and we won a famous victory through a Jim Steel goal. That was the slim margin we had to take to Portugal but, amazingly, we managed to get through on the away goals rule after losing the match 4-3. I scored one of our goals that night and I shall never forget it.

In the next round we went to Rome to play Roma. Although we went out after two legs, it had still been a great experience for everyone at the club.

Unfortunately, despite our European glory, we stayed in Division Four and that's the way

THAT'S THE VOW OF PORTSMOUTH'S
BARRY HORNE

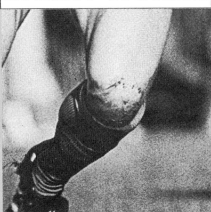

it stayed for the next two seasons, until out of the blue I got the chance to join a First Division club. Portsmouth had just been promoted and I was one of the players whom manager Alan Ball bought to do a job for him in Division One.

Alan Ball gave me the chance to feel my way in to the team and I was a substitute for the first few games. But when I made the starting line-up for the first time, I was given the job of marking Liam Brady of West Ham.

That was quite an introduction. But it became even thougher a few weeks later when I was asked to do a marking job on John Barnes when we went to Anfield to play Liverpool. We lost 4-0, but we played quite well and I enjoyed the challenge.

Before I joined Portsmouth I thought of myself as simply a midfield player, but Alan Ball had other ideas. In my first few months with the club he asked me to play in several different positions until he found out where I was best.

I played at full-back, did a marking job, and played in both defensive and attacking midfield roles. It was all good experience for me and probably helped me to get into the Welsh squad.

Then when I made my international debut against Yugoslavia, I found myself doing something different again. This time I was playing as one of three central defenders!

I think I have a "versatile" tag. I hope it doesn't go against me. Players who earn a reputation for being able to play anywhere sometimes find it difficult to hold down a regular place at international level. That's why I would like to be thought of primarily as a midfield player.

I came into professional football quite late, but I intend to make the most of it. I don't expect to be playing for much more than the next five years . . . but if I do eventually return to my studies, I'm sure I'll think the break was worth it.

THE TREASURE TROVE OF DERBY COUNTY MANAGER ARTHUR COX

THE COX COLLECTION

● KEVIN KEEGAN — an example to follow.

● PETER SHILTON — setting a high standard.

● **Some footballers keep programmes from matches in which they have played. Others collect jerseys they've swopped with opponents.**

It's unusual, however, for a manager to build up such a collection. Which makes Derby County team boss Arthur Cox something of an exception.

Neatly stored in his home is a pile of club and international jerseys, each washed, ironed and folded with loving care.

Every one tells the story of a remarkable individual performance by the player who wore it, or of the rise to stardom of a former protege, or of an exemplary career held up as an example to any youngster.

Cox's collection includes shirts worn by great stars such as Kevin Keegan, Peter Shilton and Billy Bremner.

Others may not have been so familiar to the general footballing public. But, as Arthur says, "Every one is a household name in my home."

Cox has gathered his cherished mementoes during a 30-year career in coaching and management which has taken him from Coventry City to Derby, via Walsall, Aston Villa, Preston North End, Halifax Town, Sunderland, Chesterfield and Newcastle United.

The remarkable thing about his treasure trove is that it consists of only 15 jerseys. But that's what makes it so special to him.

To merit a place in the Cox collection, a shirt must represent something truly outstanding.

Says Arthur, "I don't collect jerseys willy-nilly. By adding to them indiscriminately I would simply devalue the memories evoked by each one.

"As it is, whenever I open the cupboard and pick up a particular jersey, I can recall every detail about its significance.

"If it marks a player's performance in a match, I can still hear the crowd cheering. I remember every aspect of his contribution to the game. I can even see the smile on his face as he left the field at the end."

The jersey which began it all was the first England Under-23 jersey of Allan Clarke, the former Leeds United goalscorer now manager of Barnsley.

"I had Allan under my wing when he was a young boy at Walsall, and watched him develop into a fine player," Arthur goes on.

"It gave me a great deal of pleasure to see him make the grade and when he won that first honour, he gave me his jersey as a memento.

"Not that I deliberately set out to build up a collection of jerseys at that time. It was just something which developed gradually.

"Many of the players whose jerseys feature in my collection were youngsters I helped in the early stages of their careers.

"It has given me great satisfaction to

Peter Shilton during Derby's League fixture against Newcastle United at St James Park last season.

"I had to take his jumper that day simply because Peter had just completed the most incredible exhibition of goalkeeping," says Arthur.

"I'm sure everyone who attended that match would agree. Geordies don't hand out praise lightly, but everybody in the ground clapped Peter off the field at the end of the game.

"I had never witnessed a better display, and I'm convinced Peter achieved a standard which he will not have surpassed even in his great career."

Surprisingly there is a jersey among Cox's souvenirs which has nothing to do with football. One which had been paraded by a baseball player!

"I was able to obtain that one during a tour of the United States with Aston Villa back in 1968," Arthur recalls.

"The special achievement connected with that shirt is that Hank Aaron, who played for Atlanta, chalked up the highest number of home runs ever recorded."

Jerseys don't take up the entire Cox collection, however.

He goes on, "I have one of the gloves worn by Sunderland goalkeeper Jim Montgomery in the 1973 FA Cup Final. There are a few odd boots which scored memorable goals, plus hats and scarves given to me by fans at the end of a great game.

"But the one thing which characterises my collection is that no single object means more to me than any of the others.

"In their own way, each has its own special significance. It's a very private thing. The whole lot wouldn't mean as much to anyone else as it means to me. And that's something which money can't buy.

"If there's one memory which typifies my collection, it's the relationship I enjoyed with Kevin Keegan. I have the jersey he wore during his last League match for Newcastle.

"Kevin's dedication and the way he played the game stood for everything I have ever tried to instil into my players. The way he trained and conducted himself off the field was an example every player should follow," enthuses Arthur Cox.

"On the pitch, he gave every ounce of himself to provide the public with as much entertainment as he could.

"That's how it should be. The game belongs to the fans, and I suppose that's one of the reasons I have built my store of personal trophies.

"It's the sort of thing a fan would do. And that's what I am — a football fan. I've always enjoyed a good relationship with supporters because basically I'm one of them and they know that I work for them," explains Arthur.

"The fact that I earn my living from the game is a bonus and a very great honour."

Arthur Cox will continue to build his collection. But if it takes two, maybe three, years to add another jersey he won't mind.

Because the standard of achievement will have to be very high to satisfy Arthur Cox that the jersey is worthy of a place in his remarkable collection.

watch them turn into great players, and if I've been able to make some small contribution to their development, then I've been very happy to do so.

"Phil Parkes was an up-and-coming goalkeeper when I was chief coach of Walsall. I have one of his jerseys.

"I also have a Liverpool shirt worn by Mark Lawrenson — whom I coached at Preston — which was given to me by Joe Fagan and Bob Paisley."

Nearly all the jerseys belonged to players with whom Cox has been closely associated during his multi-club career.

One, for instance, was worn by former Preston 'keeper Alan Kelly, who won 47 international caps for the Republic of Ireland.

Prolific goalscorer Bryan 'Pop' Robson, too, has contributed one of his jerseys,

"A very nice man whom I worked with at Sunderland," says Arthur.

There are jerseys which were the property of Peter Beardsley and Chris Waddle, who played under the managership of Cox at Newcastle.

One of the few exceptions — a player whom Cox didn't know personally — was former Hungarian internationalist Florian Albert.

Arthur recalls, "I was assistant manager at Sunderland when we played in the European Cup-Winners' Cup during season 1973-74, and went to Hungary to face Vasos in the Nep Stadium.

"Before our match began, there was another fixture being played on the same pitch. Ferencvaros were one of the teams in action, and Albert, who was approaching the end of his career, was in their line-up.

"For a veteran player, he put on an incredible performance. I was so impressed by his display that, when the match was over, I felt I must have his jersey. The Ferencvaros coach generously presented it to me."

Among the sparkling careers represented in Cox's collection is that of former Leeds and Scotland captain Billy Bremner. Cox has the jersey worn by the current Elland Road manager during his testimonial match.

"I also have a jersey which belonged to former England internationalist Peter Broadbent when he played for Aston Villa.

"To this day, I regard Peter as the best midfield player I have ever been associated with. He had two great feet and could both score and create goals.

"There is a Wales jersey and cap won by Barry Hole, who chalked up a record number of consecutive appearances for his country.

"And I have a Preston shirt of former team captain Alan Spavin, who in his day I regarded as the best uncapped midfield player in the country."

The most recent addition to Cox's hoard is the jersey worn by goalkeeper

IT'S GONE LIKE A DREAM!

NEWCASTLE UNITED'S DARREN JACKSON CAN'T BELIEVE HIS LUCK!

● When I look back on the little over two years I've spent in the English First Division with Newcastle United, I've still got to pinch myself to make sure it hasn't all been one, long dream.

To have played alongside such as Peter Beardsley and Mirandinha, the first Brazilian to appear in League football in Britain, is something I never thought would happen to me.

Five years ago, around the time I was due to leave school in Edinburgh, I never even seriously considered that professional football would be the career I'd follow. Neither did anyone else!

Standing just five foot five inches tall and weighing in at barely seven stones, many folk reckoned I was just too small, too much of a lightweight, to ever make the grade in full-time soccer.

Indeed, I well remember my schoolmaster, Terry Christie, pulling me aside and telling me to forget all about playing football for a living.

That was one good reason why, come the day I did walk through the school gates for the last time, I began work as an apprentice printer, content with playing football just for fun. I was taking Terry's advice!

The irony of all that, however, is that just two years later it was Terry Christie, in his other guise as manager of Meadowbank Thistle, who actually forgot his own advice and set me on the first rung of the soccer ladder.

To be fair to Terry, before he signed me I had grown just a little and started to knock home a few goals in juvenile football.

In a way I was probably unrecognisable as the kid he had

once known. I'd shot up five inches in height, though, at 10 stone, I was still far from a heavyweight.

Mind you, Terry never made much mention of the fact he had once passed a 'too wee' verdict on me. I think it embarrassed him just a little bit!

Not that I'll ever hold anything against Terry for denting my ambitions while I was one of his pupils. I prefer to remember that he's the bloke who helped my career lift off.

Less than two years after he gave me the break I thought had passed me by, I was on my way to Newcastle and beginning the most amazing spell I'll probably ever enjoy in my life.

Believe me, the past two seasons or so have been an unforgettable experience . . . and

not least because I've been privileged to mix it with the cream of English Football.

In fact, things have happened so quickly that I still find it hard to draw breath at times. It's a bit like walking on air.

When I first joined United I expected to spend at least a year in the reserves before getting anywhere near running out at the Old Traffords and Anfields of this world.

Even United boss Willie McFaul made it clear that would be the run of things when he signed me. He made no bones that I was a signing for the future, not the immediate present.

Instead, I've been in the first team picture almost from day one. It has, as I said right at the beginning, been all a bit of a dream!

FLYING HIGH!

Liverpool's **GARY GILLESPIE** and Coventry City's **DAVID SPEEDIE** battle it out in an airborne duel.

Never A Dull

The day-to-day duties involved in the running of a League outfit make a football secretary's job one of the busiest in football.

John Howarth is Blackburn Rovers' man in that demanding job. Like most other club secretaries, his responsibilities are wide-ranging.

For example, Howarth ensures the 50-plus employees of the Lancashire club are paid and monitors the incoming and outgoing finances of the outfit.

All match day arrangements are also down to him and his small staff at Ewood. Tickets have to be arranged well in advance and a concise record kept of their sales.

In addition coaches and hotels have to be booked for away matches. Referees, linesmen, gatemen, stewards and police have to be arranged for home fixtures. And that isn't only for the first-team. Rovers have two other sides that have to be looked after.

Documents for transfer buys and sales have to be drawn up and registered. Numerous meetings have to be attended. That brief summing-up covers only the major duties of a club secretary.

Nevertheless, that hectic schedule has become second nature to John Howarth after 17 years at Blackburn. At the beginning of last season he anticipated yet one more normal campaign.

Rovers began the term with a run-of-the mill gate of just over 7,000. Later they topped 17,000 as they mounted a promotion challenge and manager Don Mackay embarked on two headline-making transfer deals!

An early season idea to persuade Barcelona's former Tottenham striker Steve Archibald to join Blackburn on loan had been put on

ice by Mackay. He resurrected the ambitious plan in mid-December. John Howarth's diary tells the rest.

MONDAY DECEMBER 14: While Don Mackay is in London, meeting Archibald, I remain at Ewood Park waiting for news. Phone call to say Steve has agreed in principle to deal. We've now to fly over to Spain.

TUESDAY DECEMBER 15: Drive to Manchester Airport and catch plane to Heathrow to meet the manager. We fly out to Barcelona with Steve Archibald and his girlfriend.

Staying at the Hotel Presidentia. It is owned by Senor Gaspar, the Vice President of Barcelona, and the man with whom we are dealing. Don makes phone call to him.

WEDNESDAY DECEMBER 16: Still no meeting with Barcelona negotiators. Watch the first team train at the Nou Camp stadium. Gaspar is in Madrid!

Time is getting short, but eventually we meet Gaspar at 7.00 p.m. We reach agreement on the financial deal. All parties are happy. We are given tickets for the local derby between Barcelona and Espanol that evening. Barcelona win 3-1 and Gary Lineker scores.

THURSDAY DECEMBER 17: The plan to catch an early flight home and complete all the contract and documents in Blackburn falls through.

We have to do all the paperwork and tie up the deal in Spain. We want Archibald to make his debut against Birmingham City on Saturday the 19th. His registration forms have to be at the Football League headquarters by 5 p.m. today. Time is running out and I have no registration forms or contract with me in Spain!

Telephone my secretary at Ewood and tell her to arrange for a registration form to be sent via a facsimile machine to the Nou Camp. I spend three hours or so after breakfast writing out Steve Archibald's contract for everyone to sign.

Our commercial manager Ken Beamish is waiting in Blackburn to drive the forms to Football League headquarters at Lytham St Annes. Ken makes it in time to meet the 5 p.m. deadline.

FRIDAY DECEMBER 18; Arrive back in Blackburn at 3.30 a.m. In office at the club at 9.00 a.m. to conduct a Press conference! Steve's debut still in doubt because we haven't received international clearance from Spain. The OK comes over late in the afternoon. Extra gatemen, stewards and police have to be arranged

STEVE ARCHIBALD

Moment!

The hectic schedule of Blackburn Rovers secretary
JOHN HOWARTH

to cope with the expected increase in the gate.

SATURDAY DECEMBER 19: Archibald makes his debut and we record our highest League gate of the season.

MONDAY DECEMBER 28: We play Bradford City at home. Ticket arrangements have been made prior to Archibald's arrival and we had sent 5,000 to Bradford for the Darwen End. Demand from our support so great on the day that fans are locked outside.

The unlucky fans are furious. It's chaos outside our office as supporters show their annoyance. We take a lot of stick. Felt like shutting the door and going home!

TUESDAY DECEMBER 29: We restrict visiting fans' tickets to only 1700 for future games so we don't have a repeat of Monday's problems. Arrange for work to be carried out on the Blackburn End to install extra crush barriers to lift its capacity from 3,500 to 7,000. The job is completed in a fortnight!

After that whirlwind spell no one would have blamed John Howarth if he had expected the pace to slow down. But in the meantime Blackburn have secured a place in the Centenary Festival at Wembley on April 16.

The club are confirmed as one of the 16 competitors and it turns out to be a massive administration headache as hotels have to be booked for different parties from the club. The names and addresses of every fan buying a ticket for the festival has to be recorded.

During all this, Don Mackay springs another ambitious transfer deal. He wants Tottenham's midfielder Ossie Ardiles on loan until the end of the season. Again Howarth's diary is crammed with events.

THURSDAY MARCH 24: Transfer deadline day. We arrange to pick up Ardiles from Manchester Airport in time to drive to the Football League headquarters with his forms.

Ossie has so much to tie up at White Hart Lane and the traffic is so bad in London that he misses the flight to Manchester from Heathrow.

Ardiles finally lands at 4.00 p.m. We won't make League headquarters in time for the 5.00 p.m. deadline so we head to Manchester United's ground where they have a facsimile machine and we can send the forms over on that.

As Don Mackay drives to Old Trafford, I sit in the back of his car with Ardiles and tie up all the loose ends of the deal!

We arrive at United to find a queue of clubs with last minute deals waiting to be

sent over on the machine. It becomes so over-worked that it breaks down!

Panic over as the Fooball League agree to take, by phone, a list of the players at Old Trafford waiting to be registered. Confirmation can be sent over from the facsimile machine when it returns to working order.

SATURDAY MARCH 26: Ossie Ardiles makes his debut versus Plymouth Argyle at Home Park.

On May 7th the League season officially closes. Blackburn Rovers' remarkable campaign didn't end as they made it into the promotion play-offs. It meant an extension to an already exhaustive campaign for John Howarth.

● **CLIVE GOODYEAR** *Wimbledon*

●GARY MEGSON *Sheffield Wednesday*

EXPECT THE UNEXPECTED

I never know quite what to expect next in my career. Very little surprises me in football these days. So far I've played for Fulham, Queen's Park Rangers, then Fulham again before joining West Ham. But now I'm at Upton Park I intend staying there for a while. I think I've moved around enough for the moment.

Looking back to when it all started, I must admit that I was surprised when Fulham gave me a chance to make it in football.

At the time I was playing for London Schools and thought that I wouldn't get much further. I also played cricket for Surrey Colts but I didn't imagine that I had a chance of any sort of sporting career.

Then one day I played against a young Fulham side, scored a hat-trick and suddenly found myself being signed on by the club. It all happened so quickly that I didn't have much time to think about it.

Of course that didn't guarantee me a career in football but I was lucky enough to make the grade. When I was 18 I made my debut for Fulham in a Second Division game at Leicester.

But if I thought that was my big chance it didn't last for long. I broke my collar-bone in that match and it was to be nearly a year before I played for the first team again.

It wasn't that it took me that length of time to recover from the injury, I just had to wait my turn behind Dean Coney and Gordon Davies.

After a long wait I did get the best part of two seasons in the first team but I knew I still had a lot to learn at that stage. I thought I would have to wait a while longer before I got the chance to play in the First Division.

There was a lot of transfer speculation at the time involving my Fulham team-mates Paul Parker, Ray Houghton and Dean Coney. Several big clubs seemed to be interested in them but I didn't think they'd given me a second glance.

Then just before the start of the season, we played a friendly match with Queen's Park Rangers. We lost and I really can't remember doing anything memorable at all. When I heard that Q.P.R. wanted to buy me, I thought it must be a joke.

DEAN CONEY

But it was true, and I became a First Division player. It was quite ironic really because I'd beaten most of my Fulham team-mates to it. Of course, later Ray Houghton, Paul Parker and Dean Coney all proved themselves in the top flight, but I was there first.

I made a good start at Q.P.R. by scoring on my home debut. I had done the same at Fulham — scoring in my first game at Craven Cottage. Later, when I returned to Fulham, I again scored in my first home game and I completed my record when I joined West Ham and scored in my first game at Upton Park.

Unfortunately, that first goal for Rangers wasn't really a sign of good things to come for me. I played in only 18 League games that season.

I did at least go to Wembley that year for the Milk Cup final but I came on only as a sub and we lost the game 3-0 to Oxford. However I still enjoyed the occasion.

But it hadn't been a good start for me. I was young and inexperienced and I just couldn't get ahead of Gary Bannister, John Byrne and Michael Robinson for a regular place.

It didn't get any better the next season either. I scored less goals and played in fewer games. After that I knew that my days at Loftus Road were numbered.

The chairman, David Bulstrode, confirmed that fact for me when he told me that he was signing my old Fulham striking partner, Dean Coney, to take my place.

I was glad for Dean because he deserved the chance to play in Division One. We played quite a few games together at Fulham but we also did a very unusual job together on one occasion.

That's the advice of West Ham's LEROY ROSENIOR

The club got a phone call one day from the B.B.C.'s Breakfast Time programme asking if two players could model some suits in front of the cameras. It was great fun to do but I don't think I'll be doing any more modelling. I'm quite happy to leave that to my friend John Fashanu.

In fact John was one of the players whom West Ham wanted, along with Mick Harford, before they finally signed me. But before all that I had to prove myself at Fulham after being rejected by Rangers.

I needed to rebuild my confidence and Fulham seemed to be as good a place as any to do that. It was good to go back and see a lot of familiar faces such as my old team-mate Ray Lewington, who had become the manager.

It was a risk dropping down in to the Third Division. I might have been forgotten completely. But thankfully I made a good start to the season with four goals in the first three games and I never looked back. I knew that I was making a good impression when, during the second half of the season, other clubs started taking an interest.

Watford and Sunderland both wanted to sign me but for one reason or another neither move went through. Then West Ham moved in and I knew they were the club for me.

They were in relegation trouble when I joined but thankfully I managed to play a part in keeping the club up. I scored some important goals including two against Chelsea that helped to keep the club in the First Division.

So, a year after being rejected by a Division One club, I'd proved to myself and everybody else that I could do a job for a top flight team.

● TOM McALISTER *West Ham United*

●ROY AITKEN *Celtic*

● **RICKY HILL** *Luton Town*

ALAN LONG LEGS

Arsenal's number nine ALAN SMITH competes with MAL DONAGHY (Luton) in a leg-straining challenge.

● **JOHN HUMPHREY** *Charlton Athletic*

CATCH IT!

Liverpool's **BRUCE GROBBELAAR** leaves his goal to thwart Coventry City's **DAVID SPEEDIE.**

THE JERSEY NO

● My first season in Division One wasn't exactly ideal. Injury certainly saw to that. But I suppose it was something I should have expected when signing for Sheffield Wednesday from Shrewsbury. After all, it was the Wednesday number five shirt I would be pulling on.

Over the past few seasons that jersey has gained the reputation of being jinxed. Several players who sported it were struck down by ill-fortune.

Throughout the first half of the 1986-87 season both Ian Knight and Paul Hart had worn the shirt on several occasions. Paul then left Hillsborough to join Birmingham City. In his debut for them he suffered a broken leg which threatened his career. Then just a month later Ian Knight also broke his leg.

Prior to my arrival in October 1987, Larry May was the regular number five. He was another injury victim, picking up an ankle problem. But I gave very little thought to all the jinx talk. I'm not a very superstitious footballer and simply put all the happenings down to coincidence.

Even when I was making my Wednesday debut I didn't worry about the jinx. There were other more important things on my mind, such as a difficult game against Nottingham Forest.

Things had happened quickly for me. One Saturday I'd been in the Second Division basement with Shrewsbury, the following week I was being thrown into the Division One deep end. I must say though, that's the way I would have wanted it had I been given a choice. It's going about things the hard way but I'm sure

that it pays off in the end.

By playing in that game I also fulfilled my ambition to play in the First Division. I had gone on the transfer list at Shrewsbury at the end of the '86-'87 season. I felt that I could hold my own in a higher standard of soccer and knew that at the age of 24 the time was right to look for it.

Being on the transfer list meant that I had to relinquish the captaincy but that didn't worry me. That was the right thing to do. How could the other players look up to and take orders from someone who was determined to leave the club?

There were a few enquiries regarding my availability but nothing really concrete. Then an offer came from Wednesday just a week after we'd met them in the Littlewoods Cup.

However, I'm sure I wasn't signed purely on my performances against them. As in the signing of any player there was quite a bit of long-term checking-up involved.

When I became a Wednesday player, manager Howard

Wilkinson announced that his search for a centre-half was over — and that I had been twenty-seventh choice! Whilst this could be taken as a tongue-in-cheek remark I believe there was some truth in it.

Before my arrival, players such as Mark Wright (Derby County), Derek Mountfield (Everton) and Graeme Hogg (Manchester United) had said "No" to Wednesday. Who knows how many others had been unavailable at the time the club was showing interest? Getting the player you want can prove difficult. Either there's a problem regarding money, the player is under contract or just doesn't want to move.

I suppose you could say the jinxed number five shirt had struck again. Nobody wanted to fill it. I jumped at the chance of a move to Wednesday, though.

I had no qualms about stepping up a division. I'd played against First Division teams quite a few times for Shrewsbury in the Cup and was confident that I could do well.

Looking back, Shrewsbury was a good place to learn the central defender's trade. Battling against relegation was a common occurrence at the club, so naturally the back four were usually under a lot of pressure.

Just because we had a small squad at Shrewsbury it wasn't necessarily true that the players weren't having to compete for their places. We all knew what we had to do and what the consequences were likely to be if we didn't do it.

That was good experience for the competition for places I was bound to find at Hillsborough. This keeps everyone on their

BODY WANTED!

toes, bringing out the best in a player. There were things, however, that I wasn't really prepared for, nothing more so than joining a winning side.

At Gay Meadow we rarely put together a good run of results. When we did we were satisfied at those few good results alone. When I arrived at Wednesday the club embarked on a good run. Again I was happy with what we had achieved from game to game whereas the other players were more determined to keep it going.

Just as our form began to level off again the unthinkable happened. Playing at home to Southampton I took a terrific knock on the side of the knee. It was thought that the leg was broken. All the jinx talk started up again, but I was lucky. It turned out to be nothing more than bruising and I missed only one game.

I still didn't believe in any jinx but thought that whatever it was, be it a bout of bad luck or just coincidence, had now passed me by. Wrong! In my first appearance at Old Trafford, just four games after returning from the knee injury, disaster struck!

I went in for a 50-50 ball with Brian McClair and came out with a broken ankle. That kept me out for the rest of the season — two months. Fortunately it turned out to be a clean break with no complications, but what a start to First Division life!

Even though the injury was a great disappointment I didn't let it get me down. It's important that you don't let things get on top of you when you're a professional. Injuries, lay-offs and even 'jinxes' are all a part of football!

● **IAIN DURRANT** *Rangers*

LUCKY ME!

Superstitions paid off for Millwall's TONY CASCARINO

● I'm very superstitious! Some people might think that's silly for a professional footballer, but as far as I'm concerned it all paid off last season when I helped Millwall win the Second Division Championship.

I've had several different routines and habits throughout my career. Last season the most important of all was my three lucky stars.

I found these stars stuck on the ceiling of my new house. And because the number of the house was seven, I thought the stars must be lucky, so I peeled them off and decided to take them onto the pitch for every game I played last season.

In fact, I didn't make a very good start to the campaign, but after a while the goals started coming and I held on tight to those stars.

I have one or two other routines that I stick to for a match. I always wear the same suit for each game throughout the season, and I like to use the same shin-pads.

I certainly thought that my routines worked last season because I scored a lot of goals and we reached Division One for the first time in the club's history.

This is also my first season in the top flight. I've played all my previous football at a much lower level.

In fact, before I made it into the League I was playing in the Kent League for a team called Crockenhill. Not a very high standard of football but I certainly enjoyed it. We even won the championship on one occasion.

Of course I was only playing for fun at that stage. I had to earn a living outside the game. For eighteen months I was a hairdresser, which was a job I quite enjoyed. But it stopped me playing on a Saturday so I gave it up.

I then went on to work on a building site as a labourer. At that stage I really had no thought of becoming a professional footballer.

I did have trials with a few clubs when I was younger, but nobody wanted to take me on. It was not until a lot later that my chance came.

Our trainer at Crockenhill was the brother-in-law of Keith Peacock, the Gillingham manager. One day Keith came to watch me play and after that offered me the chance to play for Gillingham reserves against their first team.

I did quite well in that game, and Keith decided to take me on full-time.

I played 219 League games and scored 77 League goals in my six seasons with Gillingham. Then a few First Division clubs began to show interest in me, but Millwall were the first to come in with a real offer and I was happy to join them.

I was determined to prove to Millwall that they had spent their money wisely. Unfortunately I didn't make too good a start — only one goal in the first ten games. I didn't know quite what was wrong but I didn't worry about it. My game has never just been about scoring goals.

I really got going properly in the middle of October. I scored against Shrewsbury and that was the first of 13 goals I notched in 11 games.

That all ended at Blackburn. I scored again but two minutes later I had to go off with a broken rib, after a collision with their goalkeeper.

It meant that I missed five games over the important Christmas period. By the time I returned we were in with a chance of promotion.

One of the most important games came against our promotion rivals Aston Villa. We'd beaten them at Villa Park earlier in the season and that had given us the confidence to put together a run of six wins.

It was the same story second time around — we beat Villa at home and went on to win five more games on the trot to clinch the championship.

The only bad thing about having such a good season with Millwall was that it hindered my chance of playing for Eire.

Jack Charlton wanted me to join up with his squad for a game but Millwall couldn't afford to let me go at the time because we were so involved with the promotion race.

However, although I thought my chances of making the squad for the European Championship were slim, I was brought in at the last minute.

Now perhaps if I can prove myself as a regular goalscorer in Division One this season, then I will get even more chances for Eire. I certainly hope so.

Being in West Germany for the Finals with Eire was certainly a long way from my Kent League days with Crockenhill.

EIGHTEEN MONTHS I'LL NEVER FORGET

Celtic's CHRIS MORRIS explains why —

● HAD anyone come up to me two years ago and said, "You'll be playing in a double-winning side in the not-too-distant future," I would never have believed it. After all, at the time I was struggling to clinch a first team place at Sheffield Wednesday, never mind having hopes of picking up any honours.

But then Billy McNeill signed me for Celtic for £125,000 in July '87 and last season, my first at Celtic Park, we went on to win the Premier Division Championship and the Scottish Cup.

When I first joined the Glasgow club I knew that because of their past record it was only a matter of time before I'd collect my first medal. What I didn't realise was it would happen so quickly.

We won the League in emphatic style, ten points clear of second-placed Hearts, and the dream of winning the double in our Centenary year came true when Frank McAvennie scored in the last minute of our 2-1 Cup Final win over Dundee United. Even now I can't believe so much has happened in so little time. But, to be honest, it could have been so different for me.

I had never really contemplated moving north of the border until Celtic came in for me, but I couldn't resist the challenge of playing for one of the world's most famous outfits.

My career, as it stands now, is a complete contrast to season '86-'87 when I was with Sheffield Wednesday. I was convinced my best position was right back. However, that was a problem since the man in possession of the number two jersey at Hillsborough was Mel Sterland. He was the pin-up boy down there, the local lad made good. He had an outgoing personality and was popular with the fans. He was also a very good player!

So, whenever I played at right-back, I felt I was just keeping the jersey warm until Mel returned. Eventually I was told by one of the coaching staff that I was challenging for a dead place.

Up to that point I had played in various positions. When I originally signed for Wednesday I was a winger, even making the odd appearance at centre-forward after Howard Wilkinson took over from Jack Charlton.

But I realised I was a winger without any tricks. I wasn't a brilliant dribbler, and, although I was quick, it was never going to be enough in the First Division. Howard Wilkinson tried me in several different roles. In fact, by the time I left I had played in every possible outfield position!

My own opinion is that my most successful spell was at centre-half but playing in that position was not to be. And with Mel Sterland dominating the the right-back berth, there was nothing else left for me.

I knew I had to move on if my career was to progress, so I handed in a transfer request over the Christmas period that season. The manager said it would take an attractive offer for

him to sell me and I accepted this.

When the season ended, Aston Villa and Portsmouth both showed an interest and I also spoke to Jim McLean of Dundee United. But as soon as Celtic made their move, that was it as far as I was concerned.

Although I'd never really supported any particular team, my mother's from County Monaghan in Ireland, and she always had a soft spot for Celtic. So when the chance to move to Parkhead arose I had no hesitation in accepting the offer. There was never any need for anyone to "sell" the club to me. And after all we achieved last term there is no doubt in my mind I couldn't have made a better decision.

One memory which will stay with me for ever was my Old Firm debut. It was only my seventh game for Celtic and I was completely carried away by the occasion. A Celtic/Rangers game is so different to any other football match.

Throughout that week at the club there was a growing sense of anticipation about the game. As a newcomer, I had only a vague idea of what to expect and, as we sat in the dressing-room waiting to go out, the manager simply told me to enjoy it. But I was still very keyed up.

I only began to relax just as we were preparing to kick off — then I looked around and saw

114

that Roy Aitken and the other experienced players were nervous as well!

That was the game in which Rangers manager Graeme Souness was ordered off and I can remember getting involved in the melee before he received his marching orders.

Watching the game on TV afterwards that surprised even me because I don't normally get involved in those kind of scenes. It was an example of how the tension of the day had affected me.

It actually reached the point where I lost all track of time. I was preparing for what I thought was the last 15 minutes when the referee blew the full-time whistle! I've played in Old Firm games since that unforgettable debut but they don't get any easier.

One bonus for me is that I finished our double-winning season as the only ever-present first-team player at Parkhead. It's an achievement I'm very proud of, particularly with dedicated professionals in the team such as Roy Aitken who misses very few matches.

I consider myself extremely fortunate to have played in all 44 League matches last term. After a reasonable start to the season I hit a bad spell and questions were rightly asked as to whether I deserved to keep my place.

Luckily the boss kept faith in me and I'd like to think I've repaid that faith. I was especially pleased with that record because I was aware I was playing in the position only recently vacated by that Celtic and Scotland legend, Danny McGrain.

When I first moved to Scotland people told me it could be a problem stepping into the boots of one of Celtic's all-time greats. But I took the view that I could never replace Danny, which helped me settle.

Another factor which helped me was Celtic's style of play. Their policy is based on attacking football which suits me. As an ex-winger I've never lost the instinct of going forward. Scoring three goals in my first season was a bonus.

One which stands out came against Dundee at Celtic Park in front of a crowd of almost 61,000. It was the day we sealed the title, an unforgettable experience.

That was one of a series of highlights. Next there was the Scottish Cup Final against Dundee United at Hampden Park in front of a 74,000 crowd. We were favourites to win, but anything can happen in a final and with 15 minutes to go we were trailing to a Kevin Gallacher goal.

But 15 minutes was just enough for Celtic. We pride ourselves on fighting for the full 90 minutes. A goal from former West Ham striker Frank McAvennie brought us back on level terms and, with only seconds remaining and everyone expecting extra-time, he struck again to take the Cup back to Parkhead for a record 28th time.

But I had only a couple of days to catch my breath before heading for Dublin for Eire's European Championship preparations along with team-mates Pat Bonner and Mick McCarthy.

As I've already mentioned, my mother's side of the family comes from Ireland and although I was born in Cornwall, I opted to play for Eire if I was ever fortunate enough to be selected.

The ex-Sheffield Wednesday boss Jack Charlton is in charge, of course, and I made my debut at the back end of '87 against Northern Ireland.

All in all, it's been an incredible last eighteen months — a League medal, a Scottish Cup-Winner's medal and international honours, I can't really ask for anything else.

But now I have had the taste of success I want to win more, and with a club like Celtic there's always a great chance of it happening.

ON THE FUNNY SIDE

IT HAPPENED LAST SEASON . . .

1. Luton versus Oxford. Luton won 7-4.
2. Kingsley Black.
3. Steve Nicol.
4. Ray Walker and Phil Sproson.
5. David Kelly (Walsall).
6. West Ham's Phil Parkes at Newcastle.
7. Mirandinha joined Newcastle for £1.2 million.
8. Liverpool's John Aldridge in the F.A. Cup and Nigel Winterburn (Arsenal) in the Littlewoods Cup.
9. Manchester City beat Huddersfield 10-1. Gillingham best Chesterfield 10-0.
10. Wayne Clarke.
11. Hibernian's Andy Goram.
12. Goalkeeper Peter Guthrie from Weymouth.
13. Bradford City, Middlesbrough, Blackburn Rovers, and Chelsea.
14. Tony Adams (Arsenal.)
15. Ted McMinn.
16. Rangers.
17. John Docherty.
18. Leroy Rosenior following his transfer from Fulham.
19. Eddie Niedzwiecki, Roger Freestone, Perry Digweed and Kevin Hitchcock.
20. Steua Bucharest from Rumania.
21. £800,000.
22. Dave Bassett. Watford were relegated from Division One and Sheffield United from Division Two.
23. Ayr United.

● GARY MACKAY *Hearts*

The GUNNERS Will Get Better!

● **Last season ended in disappointment for me. Defeat in the Littlewoods Cup Final was quickly followed by losing to France in the semi-finals of the European Under-21 Championship. My hopes of ending the season with two medals disappeared down the drain.**

But I look on the bright side. I'm only 21 and if anyone had ever told me when I was a youngster that I'd play in two Wembley finals before I was 21, I'd never have believed them.

I've got to see it as experience and learn from it. For example, at Wembley in the Littlewoods Cup Final, we know we should have won the match when we took the lead 2-1. A more experienced team would have shut the door on Luton Town. We left it slightly open, and they took their chance.

We're a very young team at Arsenal. The season is long and tough. What we lacked last term and the year before, was the physical strength and experience to keep going at the same level right up to the last match.

This year we will be better equipped to maintain our form over the full season, and more experienced to be able to cope with the demands.

Obviously I was desperately disappointed to lose at Wembley, but it was still a good season for me. I established myself as a regular at Arsenal, achieving my ambition of playing in every first-team match, and I gained a place in the England Under-21 side. Now I have to build on that. Fans have not seen the best of me yet by a long way. I can do a lot better.

I want to improve my work-rate to be able to do the kind of job that Trevor Steven does for Everton and England. One minute knocking over great crosses for the strikers, and the next back in defence helping out the full-back.

My target is to progress towards a full international cap, and that's the kind of role I must be able to carry out. At the same time I hope to get an edge over my rivals for an England place with my goalscoring. I decided last year that I had to make more use of my scoring ability and I was pleased with the results.

Finishing has always been one of my strengths, or so I thought. But in my first full season I netted only six goals. I tried to analyse the reason, and decided I wasn't getting into enough positions where I could use my ability.

I realised I had to be more positive. I made it my aim to do more of my work inside our opponent's penalty box, to try to play 20-30 yards further forward so that I could get into the penalty area more often.

Last season I would have been happy to get my goal tally into double figures. When I achieved that quite early, I raised my sights to fifteen. But in the end I drew a blank in the last couple of months.

The chances were there for me to have scored nearer twenty. I'd like to think I can get closer to that mark this season.

It's important for midfield players to score, to take the pressure off the main strikers. We've done well at Arsenal in the last year or so because Paul Davis, Michael Thomas and Kevin Richardson have all scored

a few goals.

Where I can improve my scoring rate is in getting into the goalmouth more often to pick up a few 'tap-ins'. Most of my goals have come from around the edge of the box, but top finishers always get a percentage from close range.

By the end of last season I reckoned that Arsenal coach Theo Foley owed me about five bottles of champagne! From the start of the season he was betting a bottle of bubbly that I wouldn't score in certain games — and I kept getting on the scoresheet.

But as long as the team is winning matches I'm not really too bothered who scores. I'll be happy if we win the Championship this season without me picking up a goal. I'll know I will have contributed in other ways.

I'm confident we are going to win a lot of games in the next year or two. I'm very optimistic about the future. Arsenal are still a young side, and are going to get better.

We are still developing as a side. There is a lot of room for improvement, and I don't think we shall be at our peak for another couple of years.

Manager George Graham handles all the players the same, whether they are big-name stars, or unknown youngsters. If you are good enough he'll pick you, and that's a tremendous incentive for a young player.

When I first got into the side, I never expected to be a regular, but the manager gave me the chance to establish myself. It was very pleasing to play in every match last season because

That's the proud boast of Arsenal's DAVID ROCASTLE

complaint. I was ordered to take a complete rest. When I reported back for pre-season training I was overweight.

I also had another slight problem. I was fitted with new contact lenses two years ago, and it took a while to get used to them. In the middle of a hectic derby game against Spurs one of the lenses fell out! I managed to cope, and the lenses have not been any trouble since. I suppose they give me a new outlook on the game!

Having played that full season, I've now got to maintain that consistency this year. Once you've set a standard, the test is to maintain or improve on it. The demands are going to be greater all the time.

Now that opponents have become aware of what I can do, the marking is much tighter. Coping with that is a problem I've to work out.

I learnt another valuable lesson early on in my career. After making my debut, and then being involved as substitute for the first team, all I could think about was my next game in the League side.

Being put in the first team so early, and getting a lot of exposure was the worst thing for me. I didn't exactly lose my enthusiasm for playing in the reserves, but it was much more difficult to motivate myself.

I lost form badly, and I had to work hard to get it back again. It was very frustrating, but I learned from the experience.

I hope that's the approach which will help me to win honours for Arsenal this season — and perhaps a place in the full England squad.

in the previous two years I'd had problems.

In my first season I picked up a knee injury and needed a cartilage operation. It was hard work recovering from that.

Then in my second season I developed a blood disorder.

After the Littlewoods Cup win over Liverpool, I found I had trouble breathing. I thought it was the sheer effort that went into beating Liverpool at Wembley. I was totally drained. Tests showed I was suffering from exhaustion and a blood

WIMBLEDON'S
WONDERFU

IT'S MINE!

Skipper and penalty-saving hero DAVE BEASANT holds aloft the coveted cup.

WEMBLEY!

IT'S THERE!
LAWRIE SANCHEZ finds the net for the goal that won the cup!

IT'S MARVELLOUS!
The Wimbledon squad celebrate a famous victory.

● Just eight minutes, right at the end of last season, summed up exactly what it meant to me to be back in the First Division.

All the feelings of the season were squeezed into those few moments as I waited with my Aston Villa team-mates to find out if we'd won promotion from the Second Division.

For us, it was probably the most dramatic eight minutes of the campaign. The date was May

As we went across to thank our fans for their support, however, the news filtered down from the terracing that we were still in with a shout. Middlesbrough were losing 2-1 and, due to a delayed start, there were eight minutes of their match left.

The tension became almost unbearable. A couple of our players headed straight for the dressing-room to spend those moments away from the hurly-

and I have to say, in many ways, it was a bit like being at a new club — without actually having to undergo a transfer.

When Graham Taylor first joined Villa, he slammed the organisation, facilities and discipline. In short, he called the whole set-up a shambles.

His comments must have upset a lot of people and I could just visualise thousands of Villa fans saying, "Who does he think he is, walking into the club and

Eight Minutes of TOR

That's how the season ended for Aston Vill

7, 1988 — the final Saturday of the League programme. The place was the County Ground, Swindon.

We'd begun the day in third position in the table. Millwall had already been promoted. Middlesbrough, one point ahead of us and due to play at home to Leicester City, were favourites to join them as automatic promotion-winners. That would mean we'd have to fight it out in the end-of-season play-offs to win promotion.

Our only hope of avoiding that, it seemed, was to beat Swindon and hope that Middlesbrough failed to win.

The way things turned out, no scriptwriter could have invented a plot quite so dramatic.

The first half of our match finished goal-less. In the dressing-room at half-time, manager Graham Taylor told us that 'Boro were a goal down.

That gave us a chance. It certainly gave us encouragement. But we didn't believe that 'Boro would do worse than draw. We still needed to win.

Unfortunately, we were unable to turn that one point into three. Our match remained goal-less and, at the final whistle, we resigned ourselves to a place in the play-offs.

burly on the pitch.

I stayed on the pitch, not quite knowing what to do with myself. I can tell you, those were eight very long minutes.

Finally, a roar went up from our supporters, signalling that 'Boro had lost and we'd leapfrogged into second place. The relief and jubilation were tremendous.

The moment was particularly sweet for those of us who had been in the Villa side relegated from the First Division a year earlier.

That was the worst period of my career, and I spent the next few weeks feeling very depressed. I even went through a phase when I considered leaving Villa and finding a new club.

By the time the new campaign started, however, I'd undergone a change of heart and was committed to helping Villa regain their First Division status.

For one thing, I felt that, having been involved in the club's relegation, I should play a part in restoring its top flight status.

For another, new manager Graham Taylor had arrived and had set about changing the whole Villa set-up.

Within weeks, there was a whole new purpose in the way we were going about our jobs

starting to tear strips off it."

The players' point of view was different, though. We could see at first hand what was happening, and appreciated that there were going to be changes for the better.

We also realised that the boss didn't expect to be treated with respect just because of what he'd achieved at his previous club, Watford. He wanted to earn that respect.

He'd done a wonderful job at Vicarage Road, building up the club and taking them from the Fourth Division to the First.

That was one challenge which he'd succeeded in meeting but the task at Villa Park was completely different.

Here was a club which already had a set-up geared for top-level football. Yet Villa had slipped into the Second. In many ways, it was like being asked to refloat a sinking ship.

Graham Taylor worked solidly for two months in the summer in a bid to improve things.

We watched the training ground being turned upside down. Improvements were made to the buildings and the whole place had a general tidy-up. Things were happening which made us feel good about being associated with the club again.

Then the players were

suddenly brought down to earth. We were each handed three sets of kit and told, "This is your gear for the season — you look after it!"

Even washing our own strips had a good effect on us. We had a sense of everybody mucking in together. There was a feeling of pride which extended onto the pitch on match days as we fought for one another in the battle to regain a place in the First Division.

TURE!

NIGEL SPINK.

For me, there was also a personal reason for wanting to recover that position.

Five years ago, I was selected as one of the goalkeepers in an England squad which made a summer tour of Australia. It should have been the start of my emergence at international level.

Unfortunately, I didn't make the England squad again. In fact, I spent the next few years battling with successive goalkeeping rivals for the number one spot in the Aston Villa side.

In spite of several spells in the reserves, I managed to come out on top. But I never lost hope of pushing my way back into the England reckoning.

That was still in my mind as we battled through our Second Division fixtures last term. I knew that the only way I'd ever gain international recognition was by playing in the First.

So it's easy to see why our successful first attempt at promotion was special for me. So much so that I rated it better than winning the European Cup back in 1982.

At that time, I was a young 'keeper, understudying Jimmy Rimmer, who was then Villa's first-team goalie.

But when we played against Bayern Munich in the Final in Rotterdam, I was pitched into the action after only nine minutes when Jimmy was injured.

What a moment for me! Up to then my record had consisted of just one League appearance, yet here I was playing in a European Cup Final.

We won the match 1-0, I played well and, afterwards, was treated like a hero.

However, as we celebrated our victory in the team hotel, I somehow felt that I didn't have a right to share in the glory. It was the other lads who had travelled throughout Europe, battling to bring home great results.

My only part in the entire European campaign had been in the Final itself. Jimmy Rimmer deserved far more of the credit than I was getting.

Last season, I felt quite different about sharing in the joy of our success in winning promotion.

There was no doubt about my contribution to that effort. I hadn't missed a single game throughout the whole season, the first time I'd ever achieved such a run.

Now that I'm back in the First Division, I'm hoping that the run of form which enabled me to achieve that record will eventually win me a place in the England international squad once again.

If that happens, I'll regard it as a wonderful honour. But, along the way, I'm also hoping that, having been an ever-present in a Second Division campaign, I can chalk up a similar distinction now I'm back in the top flight.

I'd had ten great years but won nothing very much with Wimbledon until, against all the odds, we beat Liverpool in last season's F.A. Cup Final.

They had started the game as red-hot favourites. They were champions by a long way and, according to all the experts, we couldn't play football.

I was used to being written off. My first club was Derby County but I didn't make even one first-team appearance. When Tommy Docherty became the boss I was one of the players he decided to get rid of.

I'd learnt a lot at Derby when Dave Mackay was the manager but then it looked as if Tommy Docherty had put me on the scrap heap.

I thought that would be that as far as my football ambitions went. But then I was given another chance by Wimbledon.

Plough Lane was certainly a very different set-up from Derby. Wimbledon were in their first season in the League while it hadn't been that long since Derby had won the First Division championship.

It was an exciting time to join Wimbledon. Because they had just come into the League, every game was a new experience for the team. It certainly was for me.

The manager at that time was Dario Gradi but when I made my debut against Scunthorpe in February 1978 I lined up alongside Dave Bassett. He was to become manager and have a big influence on my career.

The first few years with Dave as manager I think of as the yo-yo years. One season we were promoted from the Fourth Division, but then we came straight back down again. That was the pattern for five years.

The second time we got into Division Three was a complete disaster for me. After just six games I broke my leg against Walsall. By the time I returned to the side, the team had been relegated, but were on the brink of promotion yet again.

Since then we've been on the up and up. Our first season in Division Two was 1984-85 and even at that stage people were saying that we weren't good

TEN YEAR WAIT -

but it was worth it says Wimbledon's

Alan Cork

enough and that we'd be back in Division Three very quickly. But that didn't happen. Dave Bassett had worked out a system that worked well not only in the lower divisions but at a higher level as well.

Dave had left at the end of the previous season and some people thought that was the end of the Wimbledon success story. We'd gone through a lot with him and I can remember very well the day he told us he was leaving to become manager of Crystal Palace. Dave was in tears as he told us he was going.

It looked like the end of an era but within a couple of days he

was back with us saying he had made a mistake.

That wasn't the end of the story though. After just two years in Division Two, we won ourselves a place in the First Division.

I wasn't a regular in the team during that first season in the top flight, but I still have one or two special memories from that spell.

The best of the lot must be from Anfield. I was on the sub's bench that day and as I warmed up on the touchline, I was taking a lot of abuse from the Liverpool fans because of my lack of hair. But I was soon to get my own back. Dave Bassett brought me on and it wasn't long before I scored the winner with that bald head of mine!

We couldn't have expected our second season in the top flight to be better than the first, but that's exactly what happened.

We'd finished sixth at our first attempt in Division One, and reached the quarter-final of the F.A. Cup, but we wanted more.

When Dave Bassett left us to join Watford, people thought we would collapse without him. But Bobby Gould came in and immediately told us he wasn't going to make big changes.

All the players were very keen to do well in the F.A. Cup this time as well as holding our position in Division One. We had thrown away a good chance the previous season when we'd lost to Spurs in the quarter-finals and we didn't want that to happen again.

Last season we were determined not to let anybody stand in our way of a trip to Wembley. We beat West Brom, Mansfield, Newcastle, Watford and Luton on the way and then Liverpool were waiting for us in the Final. Nobody gave us a chance. But we are used to proving people wrong.

I was happy just to be in the team but I felt even better when Lawrie Sanchez headed the winner. I was just in front of Lawrie as we ran for the free-kick but it landed on his head and not mine.

But I didn't mind — I'd won something at last after ten years.

YOUR PICTURE INDEX
COLOUR ● PIN-UPS ● ACTION

Printed and Published in Great Britain by D. C. THOMSON & CO., LTD., 185 Fleet Street, London EC 4A 2HS.
© D. C. THOMSON & CO., LTD., 1988.
ISBN   0-85116-423-4

HEADLINE MAKERS

It's just over 30 years since the Manchester United team were involved in the Munich air disaster — but no one connected with the club will ever forget that black day. At Old Trafford a special display of newspaper cuttings tells the story of a never-to-be-forgotten day in the club's history.